From the Outside
Looking In

From the Outside Looking In

A Boomer's Memoir

R. WINSTON CARROLL

FROM THE OUTSIDE LOOKING IN
A BOOMER'S MEMOIR

iUniverse books may be ordered through booksellers or by contacting:

iUniverse
1663 Liberty Drive
Bloomington, IN 47403
www.iuniverse.com
1-800-Authors (1-800-288-4677)

ISBN: 978-1-5320-0188-8 (sc)
ISBN: 978-1-5320-0189-5 (e)

Library of Congress Control Number: 2016910714

Print information available on the last page.

iUniverse rev. date: 08/25/2016

CONTENTS

FOREWORD

I've pursued numerous undertakings in my six plus decades residing atop this side of the dirt. The fascinating thing about writing is that you're never sure whether your work is reputable unless others read it. As a memoir, I voice my experiences selecting the interesting elements to shape the narrative. Inside all of us, there's a private vault that covets to be unlocked for people to uncover our private beliefs. It's an atlas to our psyche. Mortimer Adler once said, "In the case of good books, the point is not to see how many of them you can get through, but rather how many can get through to you." I hope my narrative accomplishes that.

This story is an assessment of my life - time is the wind, reflection the sail, and history the vessel. I hope you enjoy my journey. If not: two words and one finger.

1

PLEASE ALLOW ME TO INTRODUCE MY SELF

When good people consider you the bad guy,
you develop a heart to help the bad ones.
You actually understand them.
— **Criss Jami**, **Killosophy**

So, I've done things that weren't exactly heaven worthy. After you read about my adventures, it wouldn't surprise you to know I woke up this morning and THE GRIM REAPER was staring directly into my face. I asked what time it was; he replied it was time for my evaluation. Again, I asked the time; again, he provided an obtuse lengthy reply.

> I don't know; how much time do you have? When anyone turns 65, we begin assessing our potential clients to see if they're worthy of membership. You see, the greatest trick I've ever pulled was convincing the world there's only one of me. People who don't believe in the other guy or goodness still believe in me because evil is always possible because we're always recruiting.

1

> I've reviewed your resume and it's pretty damn impressive. It says you're an agnostic and a cynic - which we like. And it also appears that you've done several despicable things. You appear to be an outstanding candidate to become a member of our organization.

> And with that I said, please allow me to introduce myself. I'm a man with doubt and shame. I've been around for a long, long time and had my moments of distrust and pain.

I was born three times: once as a child from an interracial family in 1950; another when I watched Ruby murder Oswald; then again watching the blood trail down an asphalt driveway from Jeffery Miller's dead body at Kent State on the 4th of May in 1970.

Since my first breath, I've searched for the truth. Many times people think they've found the answer and they've s been shown to have been wrong. I realize Kennedy's dead, Superman committed suicide and the government's been bought. Even technology (with the potential to marry us) divides us and it looks like the planet is dying.

We're addicted to computers, smart phones and social media platforms - sitting alone, because in those moments we don't have to consider who we've become. The problem's not how we use these devises, but rather how they abuse us. Each day we create gizmos that distract humanity from the essence of life — contemplation, compassion and meditation. Ultimately it boils down to the point that when technology provides all the answers, we aren't required to think. And we don't.

It wasn't that long ago when only a few people had mobile phones (which were regarded as an object of derision); as corporate types held those enormous bricks to their faces and we thought to ourselves, 'look at that pompous ass.' Today, barely an eyebrow is raised as twelve-year-olds merrily text away. You probably wouldn't notice anyhow because you're preoccupied downloading an app that can locate the best sushi restaurant for lunch. It wasn't always this way. If the inevitability of human extinction because of ignorance worries you, I encourage you to worry.

You might call me a curmudgeon although life hasn't sucked that bad so far. I just despise society's hedonisms and smirk at the hypocrisy with a healthy sense of outrage. My beliefs are vested in irony, sarcasm and ridicule. I've gone from a so called killjoy to a loyal skeptic owning my opinions. After all, I have to be me - because everyone else's lives are already taken.

It was early in childhood when I began to observe things. It started with cartoons. If Wyle E. Coyote had money to buy all those ACME products, why didn't he just buy dinner instead of chasing the Road Runner? Was Speedy Gonzales really that quick or was he on performance enhancing drugs. I couldn't fathom why Mickey Mouse was bigger than his dog Pluto. I didn't understand why Popeye had the hots for a truly austere looking Olive Oyl when he could have had Betty Boop. And it was beyond reason why superheroes wore their underwear on the outside of their outfits. It all seemed suspect to me. To this day, I think Humpy Dumpy was pushed.

After cartoons, I advanced to other shows and wondered why Tarzan didn't have a beard after living in the jungle so long. I was sure he didn't have a razor. And why was the Lone Ranger called 'Lone' if he always had Tonto by his side? Can anyone tell me what Captain Hook's name was before he got his hook? And why did Ginger on Gilligan's Island have so many different outfits when she was only going on a three hour tour?

Finally, after an episode of Superman, I thought it was odd that the "Caped Crusader" never flinched as his adversary's bullets ricochet off his chest, yet he always ducked when they threw their weapons towards his head. And how in world could Lois Lane not know that Clark Kent was Superman when she was such an astute reporter? That's tantamount to not knowing Hitler without his moustache. These issues were extremely disturbing; however, I was able to get through the Santa Claus, Easter Bunny and tooth fairy stages unscathed, but that Superman thing remained an enigma.

In fifth grade, I learned Columbus discovered America, but had reservations as to how anyone could discover something that already existed. That was the equivalent of driving to a different area and discovering a new housing development. Mr. Magoo had a better sense of direction than Columbus because Columbus thought he was in India. (I don't always celebrate our country's racist, scheming, murderous and duplicitous history. But when I do, it's on Columbus Day.)

It was during this time that my mother focused me towards church in the hopes that I'd find religion. But somehow the idea of salvation grounded on moral behavior by threatening eternal damnation just didn't resonate with me. Equally sacrilege was the discovery that the original Amos and Andy characters were white. The next thing you know they'll say is that wrestling isn't real (everyone knows that's impossible), Roswell was a cover-up, the moon landing was faked, Bush was "in" on 9/11, there's no such thing as climate change and President Obama's really a Muslim. If ignorance is truly bliss, why aren't more Americans happier?

As a vigilant spectator of world events, cultural trends and politics, I've come to believe in the death of common sense. Its passing has been confirmed by his father (Truth and Trust), his wife (Discretion) as well as their daughter (Responsibility), their son (Greed) and granddaughter (Narcissism). The demise of Common Sense was also validated by the three stepsons: Entitlement, Litigation and Virtual Reality.

In the scheme of things, people believe what they choose to trust. I remember watching one of the classic boxing matches of all time. It was an epic battle for the middleweight championship of the world between Roberto Duran and Sugar Ray Leonard. The two great pugilists had been in over 100 contests and, between them, had won all but one. The fight went the distance and it was obvious to me that it wasn't Leonard's night.

I got up to leave before the judges announced the verdict and the gentleman next to me asked why I was leaving before they made their call. I explained that I knew Leonard had lost and didn't need them to confirm it. The guy said I was crazy because he was sure Sugar Ray had won. I asked him what fight he'd been watching and he was so certain he was right that he bet me $100 dollars that I was wrong. I gladly took his wager and sat back down to hear the decision. Indeed, Leonard had lost and I gladly took his c-note. The point is that we both watched the same fight, but came to different conclusions. I trust my instincts, and make judgements on what my heart tells me. And more times than not I'm right because I question almost everything.

After scavenging the earth for six plus decades, I've remained a curious person. Author Tony Swartz once said, "Let go of certainty. The opposite isn't uncertainty. It's openness, curiosity and a willingness to embrace paradox, rather than choose up sides. The ultimate challenge is to accept ourselves exactly as we are, but never stop trying to learn and grow." It's been said when you stop growing you start dying and at this point in life, learning something new has become a valuable treasure.

Gone are the days when I was thrilled about reaching the green in two - even driving fancy cars, chasing job titles or vying for attention. I guess you'd say I've become a disappointed idealist. Ironically, I'm more at peace with life than ever as my wife and I grapple with the absurdity of these implausible times. "Scratch any cynic and you'll find a disappointed idealist." Thank you, George Carlin.

We're no longer searching for shiny objects. We've accrued enough stuff to appreciate that friendships constitute authentic wealth. Our conundrum now is filling the void of want and exchanging that void for need. A few upgrades would be nice but are not necessary. If my Camry gets me from point A to B, does it really matter if I'm driving a Bentley? Maybe to some, but not to me. Age changes priorities that money can't buy. It's not about having everything. It's about having passion for something; for me, it's collecting words. My most prized possessions are the ones I discover for the first time. I normally read the Sunday New York Times and invariably find myself at the dictionary because they have a habit of using vocabulary that is foreign to me.

I've always been that way about words. When I was a teenager, I sang in a Motown band. It was then I began memorizing the words of the songs I sang. It didn't get any better than the Temptations: "I've got so much honey the bees envy me. I've got a sweeter song than the birds in the trees." How brilliant.

Words can be warped into any form. They get inside you and take the human voice, inspiring deeper meaning and expanding our sense of understanding. Words are also very flexible.

Take the word shit, for example. You can have too much shit, not enough shit, just the right shit, buy shit, sell shit, find shit or get shit faced. Some days are colder than shit, hotter than shit and some days the shit hits the fan. A few people know their shit, some think they're hot shit and others don't give a shit. People sometimes times find themselves in deep shit and up shits creek without a paddle. Sometimes shit just happens. There's bullshit, horse shit or moments when everything turns to shit. People have shit for brains and don't know shit, get the shits, talk a lot of shit, tell others to eat shit or decide to shit and get off the pot. Holy shit, that's a great word.

Words can denote power and (at times) are used as weapons. I've amassed an abundant amount of words and now have something to say, which is why I write. I occasionally cite others in order to better articulate my thoughts. According to comedian Steven Wright, "To steal ideas from one is plagiarism; to steal from many is research." If anything that I've transcribed has escaped appropriate salutation to the proper wordsmith, I apologize. The reason I used your shit in the first place is because you exact my thoughts better than I ever could. My aspiration is to evolve into a cunning linguist, not to masquerade as a disingenuous plagiarist.

Nothing of me is exceptional. I'm the combined effort of everyone I've ever known, read about or experienced in life. In the age of Google, only those with no accessibility insist their uniqueness. I'm pragmatic enough not to suppose my words will be widely celebrated. An old Chinese proverb states, "He who sacrifices his conscience to ambition burns a picture to obtain the ashes." To some, my musings may be seen as idealistic. However, Dick Wolfe clarifies, "Idealism is what proceeds experience, cynicism is what follows." I write so that my voice can be heard. If what I say makes you uncomfortable, then I've accomplished my objective. At times I'm vulgar. Cynics tend to be that way, and so do curmudgeons.

My thoughts are fostered from the misanthropists who've disguised themselves as jesters because deep down inside they sense that life is but a joke. It's the Lenny Bruce's, George Carlin's, Richard Pryor's, Sam Kinison's, Bill Hick's, Chris Rock's, Bill Maher's, Lewis Black's and Dave Chappelle's of the world whose perverted observations are equally humorous as well as cringe worthy and true. Their voices turn cynical misery into comedy challenging morality, conformity and exposing false truths for what they really are… Bullshit! When you can identify life's atrocities and create comedy of the injustices, you're no longer the jester - you're clairvoyant.

Like those above, my periodic rumination may be insensitive, racist or sexist. If I jest that black people smell so blind people can hate them, too, am I a racist? I think not, maybe insensitive or politically incorrect but racist? If I say the medical community came up with the term "PMS" because "Mad Cow Disease" was already taken, am I sexist? Are there moments I judge people in a biased way? Of course I do and don't pretend that you're any different because you do, too. It's called human behavior. If what I have to say doesn't irritate you to some degree then either I've failed articulating my voice or you're not smart enough to get the joke.

My political correctness is lost in the numerous computations of my meandering brain. I have a million divergent thoughts and many are randomly incorrect. I swear incessantly and often times think sardonically. It's part of my constitution. Future generations will no doubt think of me as an awkward social extremist who could offend anyone at any minute with my outdated language. I refuse to surrender to the thought police in 21st century censorship.

For those I've offended for not being PC, pardon my French, but FUCK YOU! Political Correctness isn't exclusively the only social and morally acceptable point of view. Not everyone who disagrees with this appropriateness philosophy is bigoted, biased, sexist and/or closed-minded. As thinking people, we shouldn't lose our capacity to laugh at things that make sweeping generalizations about groups of people. I understand the spitefulness behind who these jokes target and recognize the inferences of laughing at their expense. If the first words you express is political correctness chances are good that you are part of the problem.

Politically correct people don't even like to call Black people "Black" anymore, (instead preferring to label colored folks as "racially challenged." For God's sake, I'm fucking Black and behind closed doors I'm sure I've been called much worse. The only reason white people don't tell Black jokes in public is because they value their jobs. Sometimes, off-color humor is just plain funny. It's generational narcissism to change words to suit one's own insecure needs. I refuse to concede to that nonsense.

If you're a white person, your ancestors were supposedly responsible for every injustice in the world: slavery, war, genocide, bad rhythm, people who fucked up the blues and atrocious fashion statements. Does that means that YOU personally are somehow responsible for all these atrocities? Well, maybe the bad rhythm.

You've got to be careful what you say, think, and do. You can't be seen as offending anyone. You'll have to forgive me - I'm having one of those days when my middle finger is doing all the talking. You know what sucks about being white? Not much. People are starving in Africa, thousands of Syrian refuges are wandering about homeless and there's total political chaos in the Middle East while Black American citizens are being murdered at the whim of the police. All things considered, I'd say most white people have it pretty good. My irreverent disposition is merely a collection of observations of random thoughts regarding politics, race, sex and history over the six decades that I've cascaded through. At the end of this literary exercise, I come away with a sense of frustration and disappointment. Human beings are the only species on the planet that know they're going to die yet don't address or try to correct the chaos and inhumanity to mankind. George Shaw once said, "The reasonable man adapts himself to the world; the unreasonable one persists in trying to adapt the world to himself." I'm just trying to make sense of it all.

2

ROUND PEGS –
SQUARE HOLES

"I'm different than everyone else because everyone else is not me."
— **Julian Aguilar**

Political correctness is simply a speed bump in the traffic of truth and the facts have become affronted. It's a form of generational narcissism.

> "Non-PC statements are… a problem because they're indicative of a deeper problem in the way people think. Enforcing political correctness is censorship. If we believe certain racist, sexist, and otherwise insensitive or discriminatory ideas and behaviors are bad, it makes sense that we want to stop them. If forcing people to use specific terminology or avoid certain conversation topics, we're going about it all wrong. Staying "politically correct" is not medicine for the problems that exist—it's a Band-Aid to cover up the wounds." — Queerguesscodewordpress.com

When I was young, in some states interracial marriage was illegal. The notion that love is colorblind hadn't gained traction in certain parts of America. It would take a Supreme Court decision another seventeen years to decree bi-racial weddings the law of the land. This layer is the backdrop for all other events in my life, as I struggled to see who I was and how that was different than other people saw me.

In America, race isn't a daily concern for white people because it rarely impedes their advancement or opportunity. The color of their skin has nothing implicit to do with morals, beliefs or intelligence. When "they" submit an application (to attend a university, apply for a job, look for housing), "they" don't appear menacing because the majority of the people who assess the white applications are also white - reflections of themselves. In a racist world, that's an advantage because even when "they" express dubious opinions, "they" are cut some slack.

Black people aren't allowed that leniency. I was exposed to prejudice as the product of a biracial family and grasped bigotry at an early age. When you have ambiguous racial features that don't completely fit into a black or white schism, how do you identify your world when others assess you differently? I've been the recipient of camouflaged bigotry do to the vagueness of my appearance. I'm many things because I'm a pigment of my own imagination. However, the rest of my family was self-evident.

My step-brother, Millard, was the product of mom's first marriage and was several years my senior. He inherited mom's white features and had light wavy brown hair. My other brother (Christopher) was more of a chocolate hue and I had the color of someone who looked tan but not Black.

When I was young, my family lived in a section of Cleveland where the schools were in disarray. The School

Board exacerbated the problem by enabling "selective" transfers, which meant that white students were permitted to change schools if their district was "too colored." When the opportunity presented itself, my family moved from the inner city to a neighborhood adjacent to the very affluent suburb of Shaker Heights. We participated in the historic Ludlow Community experiment.

The Ludlow Association was created to defuse tension between the races as black families began moving into the suburbs. Ludlow was a predominantly white community of nearly 500 homes in 1955. Minorities began to move into the area and integrated the suburb by 1959 to include 80 black families. Moving there didn't make it easier; one of the homes of a Black family was bombed.

Just weeks after moving into the area, Mom took Chris and me for a haircut. My mom (Virginia) was bi-racial. She was a housewife an extremely curious person and followed the politics of the day with the uncanny knack of forecasting the outcome. She constantly reminded me of a Joseph Brodsky saying. "Life—the way it really is—is a battle not between good and bad, but between bad and worse." While she was a gracious person and had a wicked sense of humor, she observed life from the dark side. Only her skepticism saved her from being an atheist. (I'm grateful I inherited her distrustful mind because I evolved into an unwavering cynic.)

Anyway, the barber shop was located in a Hungarian neighborhood near our new home. She told us to wait outside. After a short conversation, she gestured for us to come inside but once there, the owner decided he didn't want our business. I'm sure it had nothing to do with how different we looked than mom. Immediately, mom went ballistic and began swearing at the barber like a drunken sailor. She was livid. I'd never seen her so angry and didn't know she owned such a salty tongue.

After she had her say, she grabbed us and we abruptly left the premises never to return again.

In retrospect, I realize that this was my first brush with discrimination. My father (Damon) was Negro. (The label "Black" at the time was considered offensive.) He was a thoughtful, passive man with a positive outlook on life and usually sported a smile on his light chocolate-colored face. Dad lived by the "Golden Rule" and engaged people with respect. His politics were based on common sense; he arbitrated matters on the validity of their merits. But back to being judged on your color. Days later, Dad took us to the barber shop in our old neighborhood where we were accepted.

Politics inside the Black barbershops allowed Black men to gather and speak freely. The businesses were utilitarian. They play a central role in African American life. The hair stylist's facilitated their clientele as analysts, sports mavens, fashion consultants and experts on current events from a minority perspective. All you had to do was ask them because they had an opinion on everything. Old men would gather in the back room to play checkers and cards which served as a sanctuary for folks to hang out. I enjoyed my visits to the shop as I grew older.

What I learned from the discriminating Hungarian barber was that people who divide the world into 'Us' and 'Them' never consider they may be someone else's 'Them.' Such is the paradigm of prejudice and those were the attitudes in the 1950s.

What's nice about your seminal years is that you're unsullied by racial politics. Friendships develop beyond appearance. It's one of the magic periods of life because shortly thereafter, we put our toys away; puberty rears its ugly head with pimples and sexual confusion. The day we begin worrying about the future is the day the innocence ends.

And it did end, because in spite of my youth I grappled with the civil rights movement. Negroes (not called Black as it was considered degrading—Black power was a few years away) had grown wary of being treated as second class citizens. They felt imperiling their lives defending freedom on the other side of the world meant they shouldn't be deprived of those same rights at home. Colored people (which was a slightly-more acceptable term than Black) were victimized in employment, education and housing.

Although Shaker Heights was an integrated community, there were certain neighborhoods where people of color couldn't purchase a home. There were nine elementary schools in the district and seven were entirely white. There was also one recreational facility that was inaccessible to Blacks.

As luck would have it, my White friend Richard owned a pass to the segregated recreational center and loaned it to me because he was going to Europe for the summer. This afforded me an opportunity to "slip through the cracks" and meet people I wouldn't have met until years later. I enjoyed my summer by the pool and can happily say I incurred no problems with any of my new acquaintances.

Puberty hit so I had some distractions. But, this was also a time when I was trying to embrace my blackness with white people's anxiety and make sense of the two. I thought about how skin color outlined opportunity. I sought peer approval and was surprisingly validated when my classmates elected me class president of my junior high.

That same year, race riots exploded in Cleveland resulting in the city's most explosive racial incidents in history. After the dust had cleared, four people had died and dozens were injured as well as millions of dollars in property were destroyed. Ironically, only months later, Carl Stokes was elected the first black mayor in the history of a major city in the United States. Imagine that?

At this moment in time my friends and I were finding our way as teenagers. There were two junior highs in our school district. One was successfully integrated and the other entirely segregated with one high school accommodating them both. During the mid-60s, a sociopolitical division existed among Black people concerning civil rights. One faction recognized Martin Luther King's non-violent approach and the other embraced the more aggressive tactics of Black Power. Many Black students were divided between the two, which created discord at times.

Meanwhile, whites from the segregated junior high embraced integration by ignoring minorities completely. It was relatively easy to do because classes were designed by a level system. Several of the minority students tested below their white classmates and were assigned courses a level below them. However, I was uniquely positioned to hang out with everyone having visited the segregated junior high through an exchange program as class president. I also had friends that I met at the recreational facility as well as competing against their school in sports. Through those circumstances, I met two people who became my lifelong friends.

The first was Robert — who was Jewish except he didn't know it. Religion to him was what color was to me; irrelevant. We met as athletic competitors. He's the type of guy that what you see is what you got. Whenever we competed, my black teammates trashed talked to our opponents to try to intimidate them. Robert didn't take shit from anyone, which is what I admired about him. As time passed, we gravitated towards each other.

He was from a prosperous family, but you'd never know it. His dad owned a steel company but they lived modestly. Robert's father was always kind to me. His mom was an unadulterated character and treated me as if I was one of her sons. At the time a television show "I Spy" featured a detective team of a Black guy and White guy. One of the stars was Bill Cosby. Robert's mom liked to think that our friendship mimicked the characters on that program. (Fortunately, she never met Cosby and wasn't subjected to his peculiar predilections.)

Robert and I were inseparable during our high school years. He was the handsome captain of the football team and all the girls loved him. His problem was that he didn't have a female decoder ring. But he was so attractive it didn't matter.

My other friend, Casey, was entirely different than Robert. The glue to our alliance was our equally shared sardonic view of life. We both championed non-conformist beliefs. Our mantra was to expect the worst because you'll never be disappointed. We didn't see our glass as half full we thought it was just too tall without enough ice. Casey earned the distinction of being "head" of our football team without officially being captain.

Casey and I were both Timothy Leary disciples. I admired Casey for his quick wit, keen assessments and crooked political opinions. He reeked of smugness, yet everyone conceded he was the brightest guy in the room. Neither Casey nor I cared about collecting friends, but I was on his short list. We enjoyed each other's company and I was a frequent dinner guest throughout high school.

I think I got along with different types of people because I hung out with everyone regardless of color, which at that time was politically incorrect. Casey also came from a "well-heeled" family, similar to Robert. Casey's dad belonged to a country club where I was fortunate enough to play golf on numerous occasions due to his largess. We had enough in common to hang out but weren't so similar that we bored one another.

Outside of the jocks, the band and drama club, little effort was made by other Black students to assimilate culturally. It was very apparent by the seating arrangements in the cafeteria.

Integrated tables were virtually nonexistent. I was one of the few that didn't toe the line. I circulated with my Black friends from the neighborhood, white friends from class and my teammates on the football team. Race didn't register into my daily considerations.

I was aligned with a myriad of people, and sometimes it irritated some of the new Black kids where they even considered me an "Uncle Tom." I was invariably pressured to justify my blackness by rejecting certain white friends. To some Blacks, I was not being a true brother because I wasn't hanging with my homies. The peer pressure was at times taxing; however, my response to their disdain was simple. My critics interpreted my association with white guys, particularly Robert and Casey, on the basis of racial preference.

But friendship has nothing to do with the color of your skin. Even Muhammad Ali knew how difficult it was when you were always fighting someone. "Friendship is the hardest thing in the world to explain. It's not something you learn in school. But if you haven't learned the meaning of friendship, you really haven't learned anything." The Jewish people have a term, "Mishpacha," which means "family." It implies the existence of an authentic connection as comrades with a prior history. A true friend won't ask you to compromise your principles in the name of your friendship or anything else. I certainly wasn't going to support my critic's agenda at the expense of my true allies.

As we got older and I was seventeen, people still judged me based on color. I sang in a Motown band which consisted of me and six white Jewish guys. We played at bars, which provided early access to liquor and numerous after hours escapades. The perks were great and the access to women was unbelievable. I can't tell you how many meaningless one night stands there were, but as far as meaningless experiences go they were pretty fuck'in good. I never had a steady love interest because more times than not, women had a thing for guys in bands and I was a guy in a band. Even thought I looked different it didn't matter.

Talent wise, my vocal skills were marginal (which to me is an extremely generous self-assessment). To call me good would be an insult to talent. Yet to my bewilderment, people befriended me. I lived in this parallel universe delighted by my notoriety but repulsed by the misguided adulation. I just wasn't deserving. I was a teenager struggling with my racial identity while people engaged me to further their own status. Many of my black friends faced real discrimination and I was the subject of this weird admiration that only fueled my own skepticism.

The night Martin Luther King was assassinated, I was at band practice. Someone interrupted rehearsal to give us the news. We stood silently stunned, digesting what we'd just heard. Everyone turned to me for my thoughts—after all, I was the authority on all things "Black" because I was the band's only Black member. Suddenly, I was the voice of civil rights. I assumed his death would bring about violence and hinder civil rights because he commanded such a large following. His message of non-violence, pursuit of justice and tolerance made him a respected figure throughout the world.

My band mates listened to my words and apologized to me as if they were somehow responsible for his death. I told them they should all rot in jail because I held each of them personally responsible for King's demise. Suddenly the room erupted in laughter as we realized how stupid it was they apologize to me.

The next morning in homeroom, I noticed my Black classmates were absent. I dismissed the thought until I walked down the hallway and saw it was also devoid of color. Apparently, I missed the memo. Then it hit me. Their absence was a response to the assassination. Was I that naive and insensitive that I didn't get that? Completely embarrassed, I quickly left the building hoping no one noticed my presence.

Overall, the band was good for me. I was accepted to college in the spring of 1969 which differed me from the draft. The only thing I wanted to do before graduating was to play baseball that spring. I persuaded my football coach to talk to the baseball coach for the opportunity to try out for his team because at our school, you couldn't just walk on and try to compete for a position. You had to be invited.

The baseball coach decided who he thought was worthy to play for him, he was the kind of conservative who'd fax the FBI a list of Commies he thought were in his neighborhood. He embraced the Vietnam War, loathed dissenters, sported a crew cut and draped himself in the flag along with patriotism as well as freedom and all the other bullshit that makes you want to vomit.

His 1969 world was divided into two categories: loyalists acting for the greater good versus unpatriotic activists who questioned authority. Everything was black or white; grey was never an option. He'd won a few state baseball titles and was highly respected among his colleagues. His philosophy was sometimes insightful and sometimes repugnant, but always interesting to hear.

I played forward on his junior varsity basketball team and he never permitted more than three Blacks on the court at the same time, even if their talent warranted it. To him, it was all about image. Shaker Heights was a well-heeled white community and the optics of five Blacks on the court at the same time didn't represent his community. So again, I get discriminated against because I'm different in his eyes. Before every practice, he'd tell stories that varied in theme but as a rule carried a conservative message with Biblical overtones. I'd listen to his oratory but proved to be a poor disciple. Interracial dating was in vogue at the time and many of us partook if the chance presented itself. I had encountered a variety of girls through the band and it wasn fucked girls that didn't share my racial ancestry. teenager wouldn't? After all mutual attraction isn't a temptation.

One afternoon during tryouts, the coach pulled me aside to express his concern about the girls he'd heard I was dating. He asked if their parents were aware of my relationship with them. I found it peculiar this should concern him. Then it hit me—optics! The notion that one of his players was socially incorrect by challenging the societal norm in his world was an indictment on him as a coach. He not so tactfully advised me to consider amending my behavior because he considered it politically incorrect.

I took his suggestion as an affront, but I faced possible consequences for my actions. Without hesitation I said, "I won't compromise my conduct to yield to your agenda because it has nothing to do with baseball." Later that day, I was dropped from the team. It was the first time I considered being on the outside looking in because of my convictions, yet looking back, I realize that I've always been the round peg perusing square holes. "To be successful, you have to be one of three bees - the queen bee, the hardest working bee, or the bee that doesn't fit in. The first one's success is inherited, and the next one is earned while the last one is self-sought, self-served, and happens on its own terms." (Suzy Kassem makes a lot of sense to me.)

Those early lessons about race, what other people thought it was or what it should be, provided a foundation that's lasted a lifetime. Many of the friends I collected then remain friends to this day. I'm convinced that collecting new friends is far less important than preserving the old ones. They know and love you for who you are.

3

THE WONDER YEARS

Adolescents are not monsters. They are just
people trying to learn how to make it among
the adults in the world, who are probably
not so sure themselves.
— **Virginia Stire**

When my life began the American flag had forty eight stars, Harry Truman was president and body bags were returning from Korea. One hundred and fifty million people called themselves American citizens as two and a half billion people wandered about the planet.

A new house would set you back about nine grand and the average salary was roughly a third of that. Fords, Buicks and Chevys littered the road and none were equipped with seatbelts while every one of them had ash trays. Gas station attendants cleaned your windshield, checked the oil and put air in your white-wall tires during a fill up.

There were no "fast food" joints because everyone feasted on the "slow food" mom prepared as families rehashed the events of the day over the dinner table. There were no microwaves or clothes driers which meant food required more prep time and your apparel philandered on clothes lines tethered with clothes pins outside the backyard.

Television included three networks viewed on black and white screens that often had poor reception. There were no remote controls so you had to get off your ass to change the channel. Father knew best and housewives were queen for a day. There were party lines, ice boxes and juke boxes. Radio and newspapers disseminated the day's relevant information when the news was actually newsworthy. Music was played on vinyl discs and everyone listened to radio on the AM side of the dial. Guys discovered pornography by uncovering Dad's Playboys. A "hummer" wasn't a brand of automobile and the perception of safe sex was a padded headboard.

It was the "Cold War" era and the Russians had nuclear weapons, however "mutually assured destruction" disavowed their employment. No sane political leader entertained the idea of nuclear attack back then, however today with suicide bombers; ladies I'd suggest you don't remain a virgin forever because terrorists are in heaven waiting for you.

Speaking of holiness my Dad believed John Lennon's philosophy "that what people call God is something in all of us… that what Jesus and Mohammed and Buddha and all the rest said was right. It's just that the translations have gone wrong."

Likewise, he did the same questioning of spiritual matters that he did of daily logic. He wasn't a religious person; it troubled him that God was such a poor money manager. It bothered him that the Lord needed to extract money from the multitude of churches when he supported his family on a mailman's salary. Even more disturbing to him was that churches didn't have to pay taxes and he did. He considered religion THE GOD MACHINE. His belief that you didn't have to go to Church to be a good person is the basis for why I don't follow a church but take the agnostic stance, though not everyone agrees in the Black community, or in any community for that matter.

The Cold War was an ongoing irritant throughout my childhood. I thought nuclear winter was just an extremely cold Cleveland December day. What I didn't know was that World War II eradicated sixty million people and the Americans and Soviets were actually keeping score. As tensions between the two nations escalated, fear of the bomb and anxiety over the possibility of a nuclear war drove many Americans to dig underground bomb shelters in an effort to survive what at the time seemed an inevitable missile attack from the Soviet Union.

Just two months shy of my twelfth birthday, my teacher discussed the big current event—the "Missile Crisis in Cuba." She attempted to explain to my six grade class the consequences of a confrontation. She talked about "nuclear winter," which sounded like heavy shit. However, my concerns were about Judy's party on Friday and little league in the spring. For thirteen days in October of 1962, the world watched anxiously after the U.S. discovered the Soviet Union had installed nuclear weapons ninety miles away. During this same period, the Chinese invaded a disputed Himalayan border and declared war against India.

So here I am in sixth grade: approaching puberty, ruminating about how to entice Debbie Williams to make out with me at Judy's party, while China and India declare war and a possible thermonuclear exchange between the United States and the Soviets rears its ugly head.

That evening at dinner, I discussed my teacher's lecture with Mom and Dad. Their explanations were both wise and sincere. Dad (always the optimist) thought that things had a way of working themselves out, which I interpreted as "the shit's about to hit the fan." Mom, the realist and skeptic, said that nothing would happen because of mutually assured destruction. I was terrified little league would be canceled and any designs on Debbie would have to be put on hold for now because of that fuck'in nuclear winter! But remarkably, several days later the Russians agreed to remove their missiles from Cuba. A nuclear confrontation was averted. Shortly thereafter, the Sino-Indian border conflict ended when the Chinese withdrew from the disputed area. So my world was back to being closer to home than those theatrics. Little League was a go, but Debbie remained a work in progress. When I attended Judy's party I was shocked to find her making out with my good buddy Larry. Apparently he had designs on her too. This was also the beginning of the emergence of the autonomous, free-thinking human being I called Ozzie. (It was be the beginning of a beautiful friendship.)

The following fall back in school an event occurred that changed my life. On a brisk and windy Friday November day during gym class, our class was swiftly ushered back to our homerooms. Over the intercom, we heard that shots had been fired at the President's motorcade in Dallas. We were dismissed from school and I arrived home just in time to observe Walter Cronkite remove his glasses and say, "Here is a bulletin from CBS news. From Dallas, Texas, the flash apparently official, President Kennedy died at 1 pm central standard time, 2:00 eastern standard time, some thirty-eight minutes ago." Even the usually calm and unflappable Cronkite paused to collect his thoughts before continuing.

I didn't know what to think. That weekend, the nation collectively grieved around the television. On Sunday morning, I watched in horror as Jack Ruby silenced the president's alleged assassin in real time. To this day, it's the only live murder televised nationally. Nine months later, The Warren Commission concluded Oswald was declared Kennedy's assassin having acted alone and we trusted the government. It would be thirteen years before the "Zapruder" film would be released to the public. Once I'd seen the horrific twenty six seconds of film and frame 313, my sense of stability and sense of the rationality of the world had been forever lost. It's true; Ashwin Sanghi was right. "It is the manner of death that reveals the importance of a man. Ordinary people are murdered while extraordinary people are assassinated." Little did I know that the decades that followed would provide even more sinister and despicable acts under the guise of liberty, freedom and democracy.

The country moved beyond the tragic event in Dallas. Just months after America's coup d'état, the Beatles invaded America and things became "groovy." It was the Age of Aquarius, psychedelic rock, hallucinogenic drugs, long hair, bell bottoms and alternative lifestyles. Free love reigned while my other head, "Ozzie," began provoking sexual thoughts. "Turn on, tune in, and drop out" was less an invitation to get high and more a call to investigate. Conventional thinking was under attack, leaving its fingerprints on values forever.

Immersed in puberty during this time of miniskirts and discotheques, my time was consumed by sports and trying to decode the opposite sex (even if it never worked out with Debbie). I was susceptible to any whim or passion my hormones prescribed. My mistake was believing that sex and love were synonymous. It never occurred to me that I was essentially just a horny teenager. I thought a lot about Woody Allen's comment, "The difference between sex and love is that sex relieves tension and love causes it." The fact I thought about it didn't mean I understood it. My passion was muddied by hormones and like any teenage boy, I was in the embryonic stage of "Dick Logic" — where that other head begins to dictate the agenda.

As the seasons changed, murders did not. During the summer, Bobby Kennedy and Martin Luther King were assassinated, Hendrix released "Electric Ladyland," the Beatles made "The White Album," "Yippies" wreaked havoc at the Democratic Convention and the Republicans nominated Richard Nixon. The country was in turmoil. The Black Panthers bought guns with thoughts of killing the police. Race riots exploded across America and the conflict in Southeast Asia was escalating.

It was also the year the U.S. massacred 347 civilians in My Lai and Americans began assessing the Vietnam War as a wasted effort. No matter what the government told us they were doing there because 47,000 people don't die in a "conflict" - everyone looked at this as a War. The idea of wearing a camouflage uniform in Southeast Asia curdled my balls because I couldn't stomach the thought of killing anyone. Just as disturbing was the thought of someone killing me. The antiwar movement was awash with protests marches, but my world was OK. At least, for now.

Writing this now, years later, I think about when I joined Facebook and was showered with requests to friend people, I noticed they were "new" and not the old buddies. They fashioned successful online fictions about themselves. I don't need the illusory sense of being LIKED. I experienced that before. Some relationships are better left a memory. The people who wanted to "friend me" were those I had forgotten for a reason. We weren't friends in the first place, just acquaintances with memories. It's not about who you've known the longest; it's about keeping in touch.

As of this writing Casey, Robert and I remain close friends who by chance met and by choice stayed close. Friendship isn't about being inseparable, it's about being separated, and knowing nothing will change. From being pals in those wonder years, even though we've evolved and found our places in the world we've remained close. We can honestly say "I love you" and not think twice about how it's taken. They really matter and the three of us share a bond of friendship which resides beyond labels and race. This is not to say we don't see color because you'd have to have achromatopsia not to. People are like M&Ms; their shell comes in several colors but the chocolate on the inside tastes the same.

4

TIN SOLDIERS

There's battle lines being drawn. Nobody's right if everybody's wrong. Young people speaking their mind. Getting so much resistance from behind.
— **Buffalo Springfield**

On the first day of the last month of the decade, I resided in Clark Hall with a couple hundred freshman at Kent State University. I went to college for several reasons. (In hindsight if I had it to do over again, I would've become a plumber because everyone takes a shit, which ensures lifetime employment. But that's another story.) One was because it was engrained in my head that in order to succeed in life, you had to acquire a college degree. In my community, over 90% of my classmates went on to higher institutions of learning.

Another reason I went to college was that my band wanted to stay together to finance our way through school. The most convenient university was Kent State because it was 35 miles from Cleveland. However, the final and most significant motive to further my education was that I was averse to dying in a war that posed no direct threat to me, America or to the freedoms Americans enjoyed.

At that time, it was mandatory to register for military service. They say that timing is everything and as luck would have it, the United States was heavily invested in murdering colored people in Southeast Asia to make corporate America a shit-load of money. I had no interest joining the military to travel to foreign places and meet exotic people to murder.

The United States had meddled in Vietnam for quite some time. They aided the French, who struggled to maintain control of their colony, and by 1954 they yielded territory north of the 17th parallel to the communists. So we deployed Green Berets to assist in combating Communist guerrillas. By 1963, we assigned 16,000 military advisers.

In August 1964, the Pentagon claimed two attacks on U.S. ships by the North Vietnamese in the Tonkin Gulf region threatened American security. President Johnson immediately escalated the conflict with air strikes against North Vietnam. This incident resulted in Congress passing the Gulf of Tonkin Resolution, which became Johnson's legal excuse for deploying conventional forces and open warfare against North Vietnam.

The United States adopted a foreign policy called the Domino Theory. It implied that if Vietnam became Communist then Cambodia, Laos, Thailand, Malaysia, Singapore would fall like dominoes into Communist influence. I thought that policing the world and holding nations at gunpoint for opposing our interests was both duplicitous and sheer insanity. But what did I know — I was just a dopey eighteen year old six months out of high school.

So with Vietnam as the backdrop, I was a freshman in college which was a composite of dorm activities, lectures, studying, parties, chasing women and drinking. I tried to say no to alcohol, but it just wouldn't listen. To make ends meet,

many of us donated blood for beer money. Then we'd
night. There was usually too much blood in my alcohol syst
and most of us wore our hang overs as proudly as we did our
school's colors. I guess you call it a freshman's rite of passage.

My time at Clark Hall was the first time I took sole custody
of my life. My idea of preparing for the future was buying two
cases of beer instead of one. I don't remember many of the
classes, but I do recall the times hanging out late at night when
a paper was due the next day and spending money I didn't have
drinking. Somehow, I got the assignments done.

Maintaining good grades was crucial because of the draft.
Taking exams consisted of cliff notes, all-nighters and the
people seated next to me during the test. So many of them were
way smarter than me. With all that knowledge surrounding
me, it felt like I was on intellectual welfare. Little did I know
that college would become one the most traumatic times of my
early life. If you want instruction and an education, go to the
library and navigate the Dewey decimal system. If you wanted
stay alive you better get good grades to stay in school because
it was one of the few deferments from going to Vietnam.

Shortly after dinner that ominous December evening, my
colleagues gathered in the lounge to listen to the lottery draft.
For the first time in twenty-seven years, the Selective Service
conducted a drawing to determine the order for induction for
1970: anyone born between January 1, 1944 and December
31, 1950 qualified. As bad luck would have it, I was an eligible
candidate. So here I am in college as anti-war protests are
reaching their zenith and I could be drafted to fight for a cause
I didn't consider legitimate. I was old enough to risk my life
in combat, but not old enough to vote —where's the equity
in that?

There were 366 plastic capsules containing birth dates that
were drawn to assign order of call to all men within the 18-26

.95 pulled would be called to report for
Uncle Sam had a list of all eligible soldiers
litary and I was among them. By enlisting
might be assigned to the Marines, Air Force
possibly avoiding Vietnam). However, the guys
toni~   control of their eventual destination. I found it
ironic that my birthday could possibly decide when I might die.

Many of us chose to avoid the draft by attending college
as a deferment, but not everyone. People of pedigree (or a
substantial bank account) had alternative options. Local draft
boards were known for corruption and that was one of the
biggest criticisms of the process. Many deferments were granted
for arbitrary, economic and political reasons. Protesting was as
much about fighting an unjust war as it was about forcing
people into military service who had no say in participating.
Looking back from today's perspective. I think people need
to know what people who call themselves patriots were doing
back then. Dick Cheney managed deferment once in '63 to
attend community college after failing at Yale. A year later he
got married and received another deferment. The next year the
ban on drafting married men with no children was lifted and
he was too old to be drafted. (I will say the internet is great for
digging up some facts and pointing to where you got them,
as that tidbit is found on www.holytaco.com/5famous-draft-
dogers-who-avoided-the-call-of duty/).

Then there was Rush Limpballs, who skirted the draft
by attending school. After dropping out, he was deferred for
having a pilonidal cyst which forms in your ass crack. (Yup,
same info source as Dick.) So Limpballs' asshole literally kept
him out of active service. How ironic. An asshole got reprieved
because of his asshole.

Ted Nugent dodged the war by literally not bathing for a
month and appeared at the induction smeared in his own feces.

32

So he avoided duty by being shamefully disgusting. (Ditto. It is like one stop shopping!) Ironically to this day he's still a despicable piece of shit.

Other notables who managed to avoid service were Bill Clinton, Tom Delay, Karl Rove, Pat Buchanan, Sean Hannity, Clarence Thomas, Donald Trump and George Bush. Most politicians, almost all Republicans and the majority of Democrats were draft dodgers during wartime and service avoiders during peace. Ronald Reagan was a draft dodger as was John Wayne and Mitt Romney. What great patriots and stand up guys they are. But that's what we know of the real story today from those guys back then.

I wasn't as privileged as some folks, which is why I nervously waited to hear the Draft Board announce my birthday. Chances were good that anyone with a number 195 or below qualified for an all-expenses paid vacation in beautiful sunny Napalm Valley, the home of Agent Orange and other great poisonous chemicals. This wasn't exactly my idea of a delightful get away destination.

As the dates were announced, I noticed some of my dorm mates periodically leaving the lounge. They later returned with duffel bags in hand, hugged a few of their friends and minutes later vanished into the night — never to be seen again. Others were willing to take their chances and report for induction. Some scammed the system by taking speed to induce high blood pressure. Some pretended being gay, which was an automatic exclusion for service. Forty years later they amended that to don't ask don't tell policy, but what do you expect from a military that waited 150 years to integrate its armed forces. These guys reminded me of the Phil Ochs song "Draft Dodger Rag": "Sarge, I'm only 18, I got a ruptured spleen, I always carry a purse, I got eyes like a bat, my feet are flat and my asthma's getting worse."

Boxing legend Muhammad Ali refused induction citing Religious reasons to forgo military service. He said, "Why should they ask me to put on a uniform and go 10,000 miles from home and drop bombs and bullets on brown people in Vietnam while Negro people in Louisville are treated like dogs and denied simple human rights? No, I'm not going 10,000 miles from home to help murder and burn another poor nation simply to continue the domination of white slave masters of the darker people the world over."

Most of us thought the war was bogus, but our critics saw things completely different. World War II was the standard how older generations perceived the Vietnam conflict because they assumed America was fighting a valid war defending Democracy. In their view, anyone who believed otherwise was considered a Marxist sympathizer and un-patriotic.

My dad was of like mind with other veterans. He was stationed in New Guinea during World War II; his father served America when stationed in Europe during World War I. When I think about the history of Black people I have to always remember the duplicity of so-called Democracy for some and not others. Black patriotism transcended many generations except for those who were considered three fifths of a person, property and denied citizenship. Somehow the idea of Democracy and freedom didn't resonate with them. Go figure?

After what seemed an eternity, my birthday was finally announced and my number was 314. It essentially eliminated any visits to the Hanoi Hilton. What a difference a day makes! However, protests and opinions continued to rage on campus and five months later, the level of unrest at Kent would have a cataclysmic impact on the politics of Vietnam.

On April 30, 1970, President Nixon gave formal authorization to commit U.S. combat troops, in cooperation with South Vietnamese units, against Communist troop sanctuaries in Cambodia. His decree was perceived as an affront to his pledge of ending the war. Protest demonstrations ensued four days later across campuses through-out America, including Kent, Ohio.

It was a muggy Friday evening when the Kent protests began. I was in a bar watching the NBA finals between the Knicks and Lakers. From my seat near the window, I watched a rowdy crowd parading down the street chanting, shouting and breaking windows. The chaos got out of control and the mayor called the governor (which disproportionally exaggerated the number actual protesters when requesting help). Local authorities emptied the bars. The governor promptly summoned the National Guard, which eventually herded the swollen crowd toward the campus with tear gas from riot-gear clad police.

The next morning, several of my classmates and local residents cleaned up the mess from the previous evening. Around dusk that night, I wandered on to the University and noted a sizable crowd gathered on campus near the barracks of the Army Reserve Office building; shortly thereafter, the structure was set on fire. I watched the building burn as turmoil ensued as firemen left the scene after their hoses were punctured and rendered useless. The National Guard cleared the area by coercing us into dormitories as the night ended. I returned back to my apartment rather startled by what had transpired. What a riot was the night before escalated into further chaos tonight. I was anxious to see what tomorrow would bring.

Sunday morning my roommate and I headed downtown for breakfast and we noticed the campus was occupied by a large number of National Guardsmen and hosts of interested on-lookers. There seemed to be a general calm. It appeared that the bedlam from the night before had dissipated. However, the calm during the morning later developed into another ugly confrontation as several of my friends gathered in the evening in an area known as the "commons," which was a large open space where students would play games and regularly hang out. It was evident that many of the people were intent on demonstrating and unwilling to disperse. Around dusk, there were hundreds and hundreds of students and the authorities read the Riot Act and tear gas was once again employed. Many became hostile as both guardsmen and demonstrators suffered injuries. As the tear gas permeated the area I ran to a safe place to witness the mayhem along with my friends. We were compassionate supporters of the protesters but not active demonstrators. I watched as the disorder continued and wondered if they would actually have classes Monday.

In spite of another night of hostilities, classes resumed on Monday and I was heading to a psych class when I was confronted by several students who said they were resolute in efforts to hold a rally that afternoon. Instead of attending class I went back to commons area concerned as to what would unfold. By noon, thousands had gathered on the commons, shouting and screaming. For a third day, the Guard fired tear gas, emboldening the crowd into defiance. The soldiers advanced with bayonets fixed on their rifles, forcing those demonstrating to retreat. The Guard maneuvered the protesters to a nearby athletic field where the soldiers suddenly fired their weapons. When the smoke had cleared, four people laid motionless and nine others were wounded. I happened to be in close proximity of that location when all the pandemonium occurred and witnessed Mary Ann Vecchio kneeling over Jeffery Miller's lifeless body as a trail of blood oozed down the pavement. It was my Abraham Zapruder moment, forever etched in my mind.

Disbelief and shock escalated to anger as hundreds of us assembled on a slope nearby. We were ordered to leave as the faculty pleaded for us to disband. An ambulance equipped with loud speakers meandered throughout the campus to announce the college was officially closing; the county prosecutor obtained an injunction terminating school indefinitely. Regular activities on campus didn't resume until later that fall. School was officially out for summer. Only weeks later I heard Crosby, Stills, Nash, and Young on the radio sing "Tin soldiers and Nixon coming, we're finally on our own. This summer I hear the drumming Four Dead in Ohio," which became an anthem to my generation.

5

THE AFTERMATH

It is the youth who must inherit the tribulation, the sorrow... that are the aftermath of war.
— **Herbert Hoover**

That fall, the repercussions of the shootings transformed Kent State from a relatively obscure university few knew existed into the fulcrum of debate about the war in Vietnam. There were countless numbers of peculiar people roaming the campus who weren't there the previous spring. In one class, my professor informed us that these aliens would be attending his lectures and, in nearly the same breath, began specifying exits to take in case of bomb threats.

Also that fall, Quaaludes arrived on campus. The actual drug Quaalude is the brand name for the sedative and hypnotic pill Methaqualone. It serves as a depressant, slowing the brain. In some cases, it produces remarkable euphoria. After an hour, you feel drunk, lose motor control, slur your speech and become visibly intoxicated. In order to maintain the high, you swallow another pill to further reduce any thread of common sense.

Then you do something stupid — like stagger to the car and go for a drive. Depending on a number of factors, the evening ends by either getting the shit kicked out of you or mumbling to the police how you managed to wrap your car around the only utility pole on an otherwise deserted street. Sometimes you'll perform astoundingly nasty sex acts with another person (or persons) you may or may not know.

The next morning you awake to foreign surroundings, and discover you're naked on the floor with a woman you've never met before. After you gently nudge her to verify she's alive, you offer her another 'lude and have wild "Monkey Sex." If all this sounds too preposterous, just ask Bill Cosby and he'll verify everything I've said.

Doing a few 'ludes is similar to drinking a half bottle of whiskey sans the hangover and we did our share. We believed time was never wasted when you're wasted all the time. Imagine horny twenty-year olds doing 'ludes to increase their chances of bumping uglies. Let's see: fucking or protesting… which should I choose? The drug was easily accessible. The people I knew were either doing 'ludes or dealing them. No one was getting busted! This pill became was a national phenomenon on campuses across America. For the dozen or so Millennials who'll read this book, Quaaludes were the equivalent of huffing, ecstasy and jerking off simultaneously.

If you didn't know any better, you'd think the government was purposely facilitating their use. I know the 'ludes I bought came in factory sealed bottles with the manufactures label in quantities of several hundred. Could the Nixon administration be capable of something this nefarious? Hum…

His administration delighted in spreading false information connecting drug use to protesters in effort to vilify the anti-War Movement. One of Nixon's minions was G. Gordon Liddy, who served the "Trickster" in several capacities. One of those functions was working for the Committee to Re-Elect the President. It was called the "Plumbers," deriving its name from containing administrative policy leaks. Liddy concocted several plots ranging from disrupting political opponents as well as ways sabotaging the counter culture.

Some schemes were rather farfetched and later Liddy admitted to a few: firebombing the Brookings Institute, stealing the documents of Daniel Ellsberg (who leaked the Pentagon Paper) and kidnapping anti-war protest organizers to transport them to Mexico during the Republican National Convention." Liddy also admitted to mistakenly making plans (that weren't completed) with another associate to murder journalist Jack Anderson because he took literally the idea of a Nixon White House statement, "We need to get rid of this Anderson guy."

I sincerely believe that it is not farfetched and even quite plausible that Liddy had a conversation with Nixon offering a solution to resolve the college turmoil. Distributing drugs that would enhance sexual libido would diminish and distract dissidents from protesting.

As shocking as my presumption sounds, the CIA did have a covert mind-control research program MK-ULTRA during the 1950s. It continued through the late 1960s and was directed at American citizens as test subjects. The project involved the covert use of several types of drugs (as well as other methods) to manipulate individual mental states and to alter brain function. The CIA Director at the time, Richard Helms, ordered these files destroyed but Congress empowered the Church Committee to investigate and they obtained sworn testimony of direct participants.

The anti-war demonstrations and the timing of Quaaludes on college campuses seemed to synchronized to be a mere coincidence. Call me skeptical, but the question isn't about my suspicion; rather, it's about coincidences. The NSA isn't the only faction that actually listens: how about cell phone companies, Facebook, Amazon, E Bay, credit card companies, EZpass, video downloads as well as a myriad of other intruders analyzing our shit. And what's up with the drones circling overhead? Many things in American history just don't add up if you pay attention. Not that I doubt Uncle Sam but I'm still searching for the second shooter behind the grassy knoll.

This increased level of surveillance presented somewhat of a dilemma for yours truly. Many of my associates were unofficially employed by Rorer (the maker of Quaaludes) and Arnar Stone (who manufactured Sopors, a type of Methaqualone). They alleged to be independent contractors although none of them filed 1099's. With such intense scrutiny and my informal title as district manager of these independent contractors, it seemed a bit dicey to continue my pursuit of a degree at Kent much longer.

Even though I validated drug dealing by using it as a means to subsidize my education, the thought of institutional confinement didn't exactly thrill me. The extent of money and vigor now being given to prosecute students caught with dope made it no longer prudent to do both — I needed to pick one or the other. After considerable deliberation, I decided to seek a different sanctuary in the pursuit of a "higher" education. At the end of the fall semester, I transferred to "The" home of Brutus Buckeye at Ohio State, away from the National Guard and intruders at Kent.

It became abundantly clear transferring schools was the right decision. My new school's enormous enrollment afforded complete anonymity. At that time, the number of guy's attending OSU to avoid the draft was huge. It was as if the inmates were running the asylum to avoid the war with no designs on earning a degree. Many were betting Vietnam would end soon and were willing to stay in school as long as it took.

Having lost my position as district manager of pharmaceutical sales at Kent, it seemed to be an opportune time to remove myself from the medical business. Or so I thought.

Unfortunately Ohio State was literally (and figuratively speaking) an institution of "higher" learning. High Street is the main artery; 50,000 kids from all places imaginable roamed the premises daily. A Saturday night stroll down the avenue was the equivalent of walking into a circus tent with a wide array of animals and variety other carnival performers.

There were the Greek fraternities who took a back seat to no one when it came to partying and debauchery. Only weeks after arriving in Columbus, one of the white frat houses invited me to pledge their house because they were seeking diversity and I personified their perfect token. I went to a few of their socials, but couldn't imagine myself hanging with people who divided the world by us and them. It reminded me of the Hungarian barber when I was seven.

When you're the only black guy in the room, you're usually treated like the only black guy in the room. Don't bro me if you don't know me, and they certainly had no clue how I rolled. I couldn't possibly adjust enough to please these preppies.

I could never fathom why anyone would entertain the humiliation of pledging a fraternity to feel validated. Confucius nailed it when he said, "What the superior man seeks is in himself; what the small man seeks is in others." Frats to me embodied brotherhood without integrity. There's no fuckin' way I'd ask "permission" from anyone who I was allowed to fraternize with. Greek life to me would be an exercise of visiting other chapters and being trotted out as their token Black member suggesting how progressive and tolerant they were. I wasn't politically correct enough to accommodate that nonsense. The only token I wanted to be was with my dirt bag friend's tok'in a bong.

After the brief fraternity experience, I met the "freaks" who consumed their time immersed in conspiracy theories (Sasquatch sightings, fake moon landings, Area 51 and microwaves used as covert mind-control devices). Now, we all let our freak flag fly occasionally, but the crazy ones were much better at it than I was. The 'lude conspiracy was about all I could handle. Hang'in with those dudes was out of the question. John Hughes was a film director of some pretty strange movies and understood freaks pretty well with his comment, "We're all pretty bizarre. Some of us are just better at hiding it, that's all." After parting company with the people from the Twilight Zone, I gravitated to the "hippies." Their basic tenet was eternally being mellow. I met one named "Hummingbird," who got her name for her proclivity of giving oral sex. Hippies had a "if it feels good, do it" attitude, including rejecting their family's middle class values, embracing nature, and emphatically opposing the war. They often dropped acid, smoked outrageous quantities of dope and reveled in their disinterest.

Many were disciples of Alan Watts, thinking he was "the answer," and under the influence of his solipsistic thoughts like: "To have faith is to trust the water. When you swim you don't grab hold of the water, because if you do you will sink and drown. Instead you relax, and float." Even on window pane acid, that made no sense to me. The hippies existed in the land of Gibberish. They were too laid back to question authority, and I wasn't totally wed to that idea. However before you criticize someone, you should walk a mile in their shoes. That way you're a mile away and you have their shoes.

I occasionally mingled with the "Brothers," but in due course sensed I wasn't black enough to be a homie. It reminded me of my detractors from high school. Rarely did I attend black socials out of fear of being laughed at because of my white man's rhythm. However, I did engage in a few Black

Student Union meetings in order to understand the politics of my peeps.

As the Student Union meeting unfolded, I was struck by how aggravated everyone seemed relating off-putting stories about white dorm mates or negative situations on campus. At one point, it was suggested that they should endorse a Black person for president of the Student Union on campus. After hearing so many atrocity stories about Black life at the university, I thought it would be impossible for a minority to win. The White backlash vote would negate our Black votes if that much prejudice was pervasive.

I left, knowing I couldn't surround myself with people who thought in terms of "us" and "them." It reinforced why I rejected the frat boys. I discovered that what links me with my people isn't a set of common physical characteristics. It's the shared experience of being visually pigeonholed as different by a white society and the consequences of that identification. I'm a myriad of things, but none of them exclude other people because of what they look like.

Coming from a racially mixed background, I own my unique story of not fitting in anywhere and that's fine. Homogeny is actually overrated. I take pleasure in not 'fitting in' being myself when others insist I adhere to their standards. I'm content owning my peculiar space without any regrets, 'cause in this life you're on your own. Introverts have fun, too; we just don't care if you know.

Ironically, Mike White (who is Black) ran for Student Union President and won, becoming Ohio State's first Black student body leader. He went on to earn a Bachelor of Arts and a Master of Public Administration degree. Eventually, he was elected Cleveland's 55th mayor. However, during his watch, the city lost the Browns who relocated to Baltimore and the new Browns have sucked ever since. Thanks a fuck'in lot, Mike.

As I continued to assess the landscape at OSU, I met the usual variety of Robert's, Fred's, Amy's and Heather's, but somehow I couldn't roll with them. I tended to lean to the bohemian people whose monikers were: Wheezer, Faceman, Mace Man, Easy Sherry, the Witch, Bum Me Out and Mosquito. I was "Chico" to them because they thought I looked Hispanic.

Not all of them were new characters in my life. I'd known Wheezer since junior high. He'd frequently visited us at Kent where he served as a regional specialist from Arnar Stone pharmaceuticals. He was another one of our colleagues who didn't file a 1099, yet distributed their merchandise. It was his idea I should transfer to Columbus when I considered relocating.

There was Faceman, Wheezer's roommate, who earned that pseudonym because he consumed so many pills his face would contort. The first day, I moved into their house. I didn't have a key so I rang the bell to get in. Faceman passed out opening the door. It was three in the afternoon and he was on his fourth "lude." Although it would appear he had a drug problem, he was more addicted to self-destruction than to the drugs themselves.

Sherry was there, too — a free spirited unabashed woman who loved to party and thought about sex as often as men do. We met in psychology class the first week I transferred. She wore a t-shirt that said "I'm a virgin" but you could tell it was used. There's nothing more beautiful than a woman being unapologetically about herself and Easy Sherry was that and then some. She's what I call a triple threat: easy on the eyes, easy to talk to, and easy to negotiate between her legs. I'm not saying she was a nymphomaniac, but she'd been under more sheets than the Klan.

During our first study session, we discussed Freud's psychoanalysis, Fromm's concept of freedom, Maslow's self-actualization and how many 'ludes to bring to her place next Friday. You couldn't take her seriously because she would forbid it. Love needs someone to care about and her interests were based on living in the moment and having a good time, not caring about relationships.

We got together whenever it was expedient. A few of my buddies also knew her and every now and then I'd ask one of them what their plans were for the evening and they'd say it was an "Easy Sherry" night. Nothing more needed to be said. Sherry was great because she had an insatiable appetite for sex and enjoyed sharing herself with others. Sometime you don't need explanations; it is what it is and that's who Sherry was.

Nothing defines men more than our ability to do irrational things in the pursuit of getting laid. At Ohio State, there were such a mixed bag of women to experience; there was every type imaginable. One of the more intriguing woman I met was "The Witch."

Was she a witch? I don't know, but that's what they called her. All I know is that she was an eccentric woman who was an enigma to everyone she encountered. Witches by nature aren't social creatures and she was no different. She reminded me of a shadowy feline with her shiny long black hair, aloofness and nippy agility. Her garb was forever dark and rarely did she engage others in public. Wheeze was my conduit to her and I'm not sure that I should thank him or not. She was one strange woman.

Chickens cluck, camels grunt; cats purr, meow and hiss - but she cackled like a sorceress after orgasm, thus earning her nickname. I was never quite sure the she had electricity because her apartment was strewn with candles and there were never any lights on. She also had three black cats who she named Hades (God of death), Bacchus (God of wine and intoxication) and Athena (Goddess of wisdom). The witch was low maintenance, yet mysterious and another character on my magical mystery tour at Brutus University.

She never desired to go out, instead preferring you come to her place and bring liquor or "ludes" or both. She enjoyed conversations about philosophy; she was well-read, quite bright and well-versed in many subjects. After the libations or pills took effect, she was eager to get it on. She always climaxed cackling. Our relationship was sporadic at best and then one afternoon I called to see if we could get together and her number was disconnected. I went by her place and it was empty. Just like that she was gone. I was never sure whether she left by conventional transportation or by broom. She was one of the more interesting characters I encountered among the multitude of people at school.

Ohio State was home to thousands of people from all over the world but the majority of undergrads were from Ohio because the school was inexpensive and you only needed a pulse for in state admission. Various cities in state vied for bragging rights. There were the Akron folks, Toledo guys, Dayton dudes, Cincinnati boys, the locals from Columbus and, of course, the Cleveland contingent. The only thing we collectively shared was our loathing for the New York people because of their fancy cars and smug attitudes.

Wheezer and I were from Cleveland, but we networked with most of the other in state guys to form our own cartel distributing "ludes" and pot. Most of us also had part time jobs because we needed to supplement our income to pay for school. My dad couldn't totally support me on a mailman's salary and I was grateful he did anything to help. He provided my tuition and I was on my own from there. I was no stranger to work. Wheezer, Faceman and I all worked at a large Downtown department store besides dealing.

Life was pretty unassuming. I'd attend classes, study and market my wares; I'd go to work, rock out at concerts, play cards and chase sex. I hadn't the foggiest notion what I wanted to do with my life and no idea how college was going to help me figure it out. My major was education so I figured I'd become a teacher. College was just a group of buildings surrounded by a library. I will say that the people I stumbled upon there will always leave a lasting impression on me. Many were truly characters. They marched to a crooked beat and it wasn't always melodic. There are times today I remember college and live vicariously through these people.

"Bum Me Out" was a wacky guy from Toledo who earned that title because he literally bummed the fuck out of people. He pilfered cigarettes from everyone and was unfailingly rude and obnoxious. Any similarity between him and etiquette was purely coincidental. One of his cohorts (also from Toledo) was called Mosquito because of his gaunt appearance and propensity to pester the shit out of everyone, just like the insect. Of course "Bum Me Out" and Mosquito were roommates. They were a match made in heaven.

Maceman was another character. He earned his handle during a war protest when authorities drenched him with mace. He was a member of our cartel and ran a successful eatery peddling hot dogs, fries and Quaaludes. Many of us hung out at his place because it was an ideal venue to play cards (and we could eat for free). In exchange for food, we'd work the register and serve customers. His joint's motto was, "We pick the dog you get it fixed." Rehashing these college exploits may give one the impression that they were an exercise of frivolity and decadence. Others would say I can relate because they were the best years of my life. Actually, they're a reflection on youth's lack of discretion. We basically never grow up; we simply learn how to modify our behavior in public. Prevailing wisdom says you make mistakes when you're young, but actually we simply make fewer when we're grown up. Good judgment comes from experience, and experience comes from making mistakes.

Astonishingly I graduated with a B.S. degree in Education in the fall of 1973, coinciding with the time the U.S. retreated from Vietnam. I departed Columbus five months later with a degree in hand and returned home alive while 58,220 American soldiers returned in body bags from a misguided war the United States fought to enhance the riches of the military industrial complex. What were the lessons I learned from that fiasco?

For me, it was that war in the end is always about betrayal—betrayal of the young by the old, of soldiers by politicians and of idealists by cynics. Nearly three decades later we'd replicate that betrayal, replacing the lie about U.S. ships being attacked in the Gulf of Tonkin to modern-day "box cutters" mistakenly portrayed as weapons of mass destruction. Betrayal happens. Sherrylin Kenyon wrote, "It's what unites us. The trick is not to let it destroy your trust in others when that happens. Don't let them take that from you." Investigate those you decide to trust because the only thing a man can betray is his conscience.

6

MURRAY

One Universe, Nine planets, Two Hundred and Four countries, seven seas and I had the privilege of meeting you.
— *Unknown*

Imagine living in a metropolis full of magnificent splendor, allure and history. That distinction is rare and very few cities merit that notoriety. Paris, New York, Rome, Madrid, London and Tokyo are among those who belong to that elite group. Other locations get by on their charm, climate, topography, shoreline or notable past. Cities such as San Francisco, New Orleans and Chicago immediately come to mind.

Then, there are places that were once-booming manufacturing towns and have severely declined due to crime, economic volatility and general depression. Detroit, Camden, Youngstown and Flint are often mentioned. Without a doubt, that list also includes my hometown of Cleveland.

To me, it will never be a dreaded location, but rather a pleasurable childhood state of mind. No matter how much people "trash talk" Cleveland, it's the least of my concerns what others think. For instance, Cleveland once had the distinction from Forbes magazine rating it as America's Most Miserable City. I believe the people who decide this shit either never visited there, their spouses had affairs there, they're die-hard Steelers fans, or are those who hate rock and roll. After all, we're not Dresden after World War II, for God's sake. (That distinction belongs to Detroit.)

We were originally known as the "Forest City." In the 1970s, city planners tried marketing the city to conventions and tourists as "the Plum City" (similar to NYC's Big Apple moniker). Today, you'll hear Cleveland called the "Rock and Roll Capital of the World" and the "North Coast" though most outsiders will always refer to us as "The Mistake on the Lake." When people refer to my town as "The Mistake on the Lake," usually I ask if they've ever visited. Most people say, "No," which leads me to question why they trash my city. Today I live in Philly and they talk badly about my hometown. Their typical response about trashing Cleveland is because they're from Philly with the attitude as if that's something noteworthy.

However, I do give Philly credit for things that are uniquely "Philly." They have the "Wing Bowl," where they pack a 20,000-seat arena to watch competitors gorge themselves on chicken wings until they vomit. It's an annual event. Former governor Ed Rendell attended Wing Bowls II, III, IV and VI, where he presented the winner with a "Liberty Bell" trophy. (However... five-time Wing Bowl champion Bill "El Wingador" Simmons is currently serving a seven-year sentence for dealing cocaine. Nice!)

Philadelphia is truly a great place and I'm not a Philly hater. If you haven't visited, you'll find quirks that make it what homers love. My point is that if you've never been to a place, you don't know what you're talking about. I'll never put down anybody's hometown. So what if one of Cleveland's tallest building is named Terminal, the lake is named Erie and the river catches fire? Granted we're the first major city to declare bankruptcy and the mayor's wife declined an invitation to the White House because it conflicted with her bowling night. Doesn't this happen everywhere?

Many cities have beloved characters uniquely associated to their town. The "Rat Pack" owned Vegas, Woody Allen personified New York and Oprah ruled Chicago. Cleveland's had a litany of zany characters, too, such as Don King and George Steinbrenner. In the early 70's, we embraced another less well-known eccentric personality. His name is Murray Saul, also known as "The Get Down Man," and I had the delightful fortune of knowing him as both a roommate, celebrity and mentor. If you want see this character you can Google Murray Saul the get down man and you'll see what a Wildman he was. His kinship provided an indelible footprint on my life and here's how I got to know him.

We used to circle through the same groups back when I was at Kent. Murray wasn't "The Man" just yet, but he was quite the character. He often spoke about the vulgarized society we're asked to tolerate as the means of sustaining regular interaction. He also expressed how the "man" was a slave driver interested only in profits at the expense of workers. He was a steadfast advocate of civil rights and extremely repulsed by the war in Vietnam. Murray was fanatical and downright indignant venting his politics. I felt exactly the same way after that day on campus, May 4th. Although we partied frequently at Kent, we lost contact when I transferred to Ohio State.

In 1974, I was twenty-three; I'd just returned from being a summer counselor at a boy's camp in Wisconsin to begin a teaching career. My carefree life and the responsible one were about to exchange places. Not ready was no longer an excuse. It's the intersection where accountability and recklessness have a confrontation. I had gotten my first legitimate job and was out on my own. My peers were on two poles: they began to get married or continued partying (to avoid commitment altogether). I was somewhere in-between. I thought I'd be okay, but knew the path to any success wouldn't be linear process. Purpose comes with age, but life isn't designed with a precise moment when that occurs.

I needed a place to live, so I called my friend, Stick, to rent a bedroom I'd heard he had available. He was delighted to renew our days as "Kinsman brothers" at Kent State. Stick's real name is Larry, but we called him Stick because of his prowess at the billiard table. "Kinsman" was a term we invented from an intersection that divided the "tony" suburb of Shaker Heights and the oppressed municipality of Cleveland. Shaker renamed the Kinsman thoroughfare once on its side of the threshold to Chagrin in order to differentiate itself from the city. We thought that was so pretentious we embraced Kinsman as our metaphor for human behavior. When someone or something appeared to be dubious, we'd call it Kinsman. If something was honorable and inspiring, we thought of it as Chagrin. It was good to reconnect with Stick.

While I impersonated a teacher by day, Stick managed the service department at a large car dealership. My friend, Larry, was the Zen master of bullshit and guru of the up-sell. Customers would schedule routine maintenance only to be informed later that their vehicle was subject to a catastrophic breakdown without some replacement part or major adjustment. By the time Stick explained his diagnosis, customers were more than a few dollars lighter in their wallet. His bonuses were based on up-selling and, ironically, his dealership was located at the intersection of Kinsman and Chagrin Boulevard.

We also shared the apartment with Murray, which is how he came back into my life. He was a man who was twice our age and one of the most contrarian, bombastic, unfiltered and loveable characters Cleveland radio has ever known. He was truly one of a kind. Born in Cleveland in 1928 and after graduating high school, he bounced around the world while serving in the military and briefly attended Ohio State (well before I did). At one point, he traveled around the United States. Along the way, he smoked a healthy amount of dope. Returning to Cleveland in the '50s, he worked in sales and opened a men's haberdashery.

He'd been smoking marijuana long before any of us were born and had the stamina to party as hard as we did. Murray could best be described as a hybrid "beatnik/hippy" whose politics dangled heavily left. His age and experience lent credibility to his beliefs, though his appearance didn't necessarily give that same impression. His former boss, John Gorman, wrote about him in the Cleveland Free Press where he described him in 2008 as having, "…wild hair that sprouted from the sides and back of his head, and long, equally untamed muttonchops. He had a voice, deep and smooth, except when he was really cranked up about something; then it took on the texture of a gravel driveway strewn with glass."

When we renewed our relationship in Cleveland as roommates, he was an account executive for WMMS (a.k.a. Weed Makes Me Smile) radio, which was a huge FM rocker that dominated the Cleveland market in its seminal years. The station was on the verge of dethroning the AM side of the dial (where previously everyone listened to music). It was a shift in times even for the way people listened to music. Radio owners viewed FM as a loss-leader and a way to comply with government regulations. AM radio was still their principal revenue source. They never saw the potential of FM. Because of Murray's age and sales skills he was able to talk to business owners with credibility, giving him exposure all over town and opening doors.

It also helped him evolve into "The Man." John (the station's program director) dropped in regularly to the house and witnessed many of our shouting matches cloaked as discussion. John wasn't as cantankerous as the rest of us; however, he was maniacal promoting the radio station. John didn't go to work — he went to war permanently fixed in nuclear attack mode because every station was the enemy, which had to be destroyed at all costs. His mantra was all about tallying dead carcasses and his brazenness perfectly matched Murray's sardonic charges, thus fashioning an everlasting friendship.

John was also privy to Murray screaming at his aunt who was hard of hearing. Sometime later, at another gathering one of our guests played air guitar and Murray yelled "Get down, Goddamnit." Murray's voice and passion inspired John to feature him as a personality on the radio, closing the work week with a downright bombastic commentary. He was christened "The Get Down Man" because he generated ginormous rating shares ranting insanity every Friday on the most popular radio station in the city. He rocked Cleveland into a merrymaking weekend and the entire 18-40 aged population in the city would tune in to make it official.

Murray's paid tirade garnered a slot on Fridays at 5:55pm, where he spewed crazy politics and other injustices across the airways. What was an unusual experiment evolved into "appointment listening" for the most coveted demo in radio. Progressive rock and antiwar politics embraced Murray into the sixties culture. His rant was packaged as "The Friday Get Down" and it gathered an enormous listening audience. Every Friday, as radios were turned up for the ceremonial spinning of Springsteen's "Born to Run," immediately followed by the "Get Down," which was the official start of Cleveland's weekend. Any time with Murray could turn into one wild ride. There was the time he and John were having dinner with several colleagues. Gorman was into a conversation at one end of the table when suddenly Murray shot up from his seat, knocking it over, thrust a finger at a man sitting nearby and shouted, "Well, what's your idea of fucking heaven?" Whatever turn in the discussion had set him off, Murray wouldn't let it go, even when the man tried to leave the restaurant. Murray followed him, repeating, "What's your idea of fucking heaven? I have a fucking right to know!" When he recounted the story, John recalled hearing a woman sitting nearby saying, "I hope he doesn't have a gun."

I was half Murray's age when our "roommate reunion" resumed the friendship. His experience obviously surpassed mine. I was this cocky "know it all," fairly creative person making mistakes, but not yet having the capability to know which ones not to repeat. Murray on the other hand had been there and done everything and owned a lavish tee shirt collection in his closet. In spite of the age disparity, we shared similar interests because we both followed the politics of the day. The glue to our friendship was our mutual outrage of 1970's America. In time, Murray, Stick and I settled into an evening routine which we followed over the course of our union.

Most weekdays we'd return home and unwind to cocktails, bongs or whatever pills were at our disposal. Stick usually began the festivities telling outrageous tales about swindling his customers. He had a knack of telling tales that had us laughing our asses off. The things he said were too incredible to be believed; however, they were so funny it didn't matter. He had his own language that made sense, but his words weren't in the dictionary. (My favorite was "Garza," which he used to describe unsightly residue, as in, "The guy had all kinds of garza on his face." Another was "gubus," which he equated to mean junk. Somehow you understood his words.)

Murray usually followed Stick by selecting his indignation "de jour," which was a variation of something "The Man" did to pervert truth, justice and the American way. He observed life with a suppressed rage, knowing the deck was stacked, the game was rigged and greed trumped principle. We considered our conversations rational in spite of being under the influence of the various substances we'd consumed. It was equally presumed that yelling and swearing were a part of the debate format. The topic was irrelevant because we alternated championing the opposite side of everything discussed.

Murray's life experience and wisdom heightened his ability to entertain many facets of a topic, crafting one side as more plausible than the other. He had a better command of events having lived during the times when they occurred and that proved to be an enormous advantage. Most of my retorts were based on what I had read and learned second hand.

Once the dust had settled and the discussion ended, the victor would say, "Everyone's entitled to an eraser and it's time for you to use yours." We'd then return to civil discourse never taking umbrage with the vulgarity and passion previously stated. We were simply delighted having a dispute. It was in our DNA and just how we normally went about our lives.

Oddly, though, Murray was at least as comfortable (if not more so) with his other non-sales role at the station—journalist. He interviewed guests for serious topics on "Jabberwocky," a Sunday morning public affairs show and "We the People," a series of five-minute clips played every Monday, Wednesday and Friday afternoon. In these, he was nothing like the madman who fired the starting gun for the weekend; he was thoughtful and insightful, holding his own with guests like Mayor Dennis Kucinich and talking about issues like regionalism before anyone even called it that. The gig tapped into a part of Murray that he hadn't forgotten but few knew — the curious, well-read, passionate student of history and son of a city that was dying before his eyes. (It's expounded upon in John Gorman's <u>The Buzzard</u>.)

That person, the calm intellectual, is the man I knew as my roommate and mentor. He had a charming side that he rarely displayed because it didn't fit the image of "The Get Down Man." I was privy to his company on a daily basis and witnessed a courteous, gentler and charming gentleman who was gracious when he chose to be. That bombastic personality was the person everyone else heard on the radio. It was only in public that his outlandish character reared its ugly head. For example, Frank Lewis wrote a story in the Cleveland Free Times (again in 2008) about one outlandish story. "'Someone called out for Murray to watch his language. He looked around, and then said, "Fuck. Fuck, fuck, fuck, fuck, fuck." And then he sits down and keep eating,' John recalls, 'like nothing ever happened.'"

I would listen to his "Get Down," but never fervently because it was a sanitized version of our nightly unwind at home. There were times he'd refer to me in his rants and that didn't sit well with my principal. Over time, he became a sage to the city's youth who to this day consider him a deity. Never was his revered status so prevalent than when at Municipal Stadium where he introduced the headline act (I think it was the Stones) in front of 70,000 people. As he walked on to the stage the crowd went berserk because he personified that rebellion against authority which is, after all, what rock and roll is all about.

Because he was so popular, that spread to our home-life, too. During these halcyon days, we never knew who'd drop by to share happy hour. Murray collected a gaggle of characters, my friends sporadically visited, other guest's included TV, radio personalities and professional athletes. Others were people and fans who just loved the station. Murray's clients (since he still did radio sales for John even though he did some live air personality stuff) wandered in as well. Stick donated women he lured during his daily exploits. Our apartment was a web in a spider's nest of decadence.

There were times for official parties, not just "wander in off the street" parties. In May of each year, the radio station threw an unofficial party for itself because several employees shared birthdays that month. It was unofficially called the "Taurus" party that served as an excuse for people in the radio industry to party their asses off. Somehow, they were able to expense this event and what was allegedly a party became a Caligula affair. There were literally hundreds of people who attended the extravaganza. On a few occasions, our apartment served as the venue for this event.

Cars were parked a mile down the boulevard and to everyone's astonishment the cops never disrupted the event. The variety of characters and the level of self-indulgence was incredible. The party hemorrhaged next door and outside where people were openly smoking dope, snorting lines of coke and drinking whiskey directly from the bottle. By night's end, we literally had to wake people up and throw them out of our place. I can't believe we weren't busted.

It never really occurred to me during Murray's "Get Down" days that he was such a luminary. While he embraced his crazy radio persona and was adored by thousands of fans, I never considered him someone special. It was reminiscent of my years in a band when people pursued my attention confusing me with someone they believed was important. Murray was simply my unfiltered, belligerent outrageous roommate to whom thousands of people listened to on the radio.

Even when he wasn't playing a role, he garnered attention. There was a Jethro Tull concert at Kent State that we went to see. Someone suggested that Murray introduce the band and when he went backstage, we went to our seats. Murray returned to us very angry. The band had other ideas about who would introduce them. Murray began yelling at us saying the band had shit on him and he wasn't going to take it. He was yelling louder and louder, and the crowd recognized him and thought it was an impromptu "Get Down" rant. They began applauding him and chanting his name. He jumped up on his chair and ended up getting more applause than Jethro Tull.

There was another night where we dined at a fancy restaurant whose walls displayed various local celebrities. Murray's picture was among them. After finishing our meal he noticed his portrait had been photo shopped with him attired in a suit. He instantly became irritated. He ripped the picture off the wall and had testy words with the owner, including, "How dare you make me look like all these asshole suits?" He stormed away indignant. That episode was the epitome of my belligerent friend.

A third example is too good not to share. An old high school friend of mine dropped by and I introduced him to Murray. After a brief discussion, Murray associated his mother with a classmate he knew in high school. Murray asked him if she was a brunette with a beauty mark on her left hand and indeed she was. Without missing a beat, Murray said, "You know, I think I fucked your mother!" I couldn't determine if my friend was impressed, shocked or outraged, but I do know that Stick and I had a hard time getting off the floor from laughing.

As time passed, Stick and I had to weigh where we'd accompany Murray because the bedlam he created was just too annoying. There were certain places we especially avoided because fans would constantly yell "Get Down" wanting to command his attention and that interrupted our evening.

However, the perks were fantastic. WMMS promoted "The World Series of Rock," a succession of summer concerts held at the old Municipal Stadium. We went with Murray to these events which included Lynyrd Skynyrd, James Gang, Crosby, Stills, Nash & Young, Santana, The Band, Chicago, Rolling Stones, Yes and Aerosmith just to name a few. This list doesn't include the arenas or small venues we'd attended during those years. One of which was a limousine chauffeured concert to see Led Zeppelin. Murray knew we'd all be too high for anyone to drive so he ordered a limo for the night.

After three glorious years, it was time to move on. My decision to leave wasn't the end of our friendship; rather, just time to end this chapter of living together like it or not, nothing remains the same. Murray's radio career ended as abruptly and unpredictably as it had begun. Marching in a Labor Day parade in 1977, he heard a young boy on the sidewalk chanting, "Got-ta, got-ta, got-ta get DOWN damnit!" In a flash, he realized that the phenomenon, as he said, "had burned out."

Murray and I maintained a solid relationship after we parted company as roommates. We'd see each other when convenient and it was a closer relationship than before because it didn't involve all the celebrity nonsense. My affiliation with Murray was never about his celebrity or all the absolutely crazy merrymaking we experienced together. What I loved about him was his disdain for the fraud mired in a society where success becomes its own justification. He screamed about how we tolerate greed and prejudice as a part of our daily routine experience, never organizing a concerted effort to combat it. He was always outraged by that idea and encouraged everyone to "Get Down, Goddamnit." He was my Howard Beal in real life — mad as hell and not willing to take it anymore.

He remained feisty, but I could sense he'd lost some of his argumentative fastball. Nonetheless, we had thought-provoking exchanges on the phone as I'd move away, and they all confirmed his ongoing passion for life. He continued to date several women into his eighties. Death took Murray in the spring of 2014.

At the memorial service, I was invited to comment about my departed friend and I said, "There are tens of thousands of people who knew the 'Get Down Man,' but only the two dozen or so here tonight actually knew Murray Saul. During the course of the evening, we'll all swap stories about him and at some point utter these four words: 'and you know Murray,' which meant you could expect the outcome of the story was going to be outrageous and amusing." Murray's best friend and former boss, John, added, "We helped Murray Saul commit his final act of soft-core civil disobedience at his lakeside memorial... when we illegally scattered his ashes on Lake Erie." John was at the hospital on Murray's last day and said he was joking with the nurse up until his death. He went on to say that if there's weed in heaven, Murray Saul is probably smoking some. If not, he's probably directing someone to get-down and get him some.

It was noteworthy that Murray's memorial occurred on a rare full moon one Friday the 13th. There won't be another one of those until August 2049, which is befitting because there will never be another character like him until well after that. Murray died at 86 and smoked his last joint the day before he died. "Get Down," my friend.

7

DICK LOGIC

Life is like a penis. When it's soft you can't beat it. When it's hard, you get screwed.
— Samuel Shem "The House of God"

It was Dale Carnegie who said it isn't what you have, or who you are... or what you're doing that makes you happy or unhappy. It's what you think about. Unfortunately, the vast majority of men are usually thinking about sex. The difference between genders is that women want men to satisfy a number of their needs while men want women to satisfy just one. You see a penis is this thing that's just dangling down there all alone looking for a place to hang, sort of like a vagrant searching for a home. When it finds shelter, it moves in. Now, I grant you that women can fake orgasms, but men can fake entire relationships - which is why we're called dicks. Believe me, I would know because I've been considered a dick too many times not to remember.

However, today I've changed and I'm happily married to a wonderful woman who puts up with my sarcastic bullshit. Ironically, just when I finally got my other head together my body started to fall apart and my dick, "Ozzie," has forsaken me. My penis abandoning me has altered my assessment of life. I'm no longer bipolar and much less stressed. My notion of a night out is sitting on the deck and the idea of getting "lucky" means finding my car in congested parking lot on the first try.

The loss of my other brain happened a few years ago. While leaving Home Depot, I began fumbling for the keys in my pocket and discovered something was missing in my crouch area. Somehow, my dick was inexplicably missing. Frantically I searched throughout the store but couldn't find the damn thing. I rummaged around everywhere. As a last resort I went to Customer Service and asked if anyone had returned a missing penis, which regrettably the clerk said no one had (however, he did take my number and said he'd call if someone did).

Disheartened, I left the store when suddenly I spotted it bolting across the parking lot. From a distance, it turned around and shouted: "Good-bye, our attachment is over. It's not you… it's me… well, ok, it's you. Now that you're married, we don't take road trips anymore, which eliminates my ability to pervert you. You love your wife. How dare you - that's boring. You're being very selfish. Here's the phone number of my Cialis doctor, I think you two should talk. I need further conquests and more adventure. Remember the old days when we woke up with exotic women. You're way too sensible now. You don't hang out at bars anymore. That's why I'm moving several states away. Yeah sure, I'll call… the minute I get there. Just remember roses are red, violets are blue, sugar is sweet and so were you… but now, the roses are wilted, the violets are dead, the sugar bowls empty and so is your head." And just like, that I lost my imaginary four hour erections forever.

I guess the stability of marriage didn't agree with him. My wife's been compassionate about my loss because I think it's one less thing she has to deal with. I've come to terms with the abandonment of my other brain because until I was married, ninety percent of the time he skewed my judgment and the other ten percent he spoke on his own behalf.

His rowdy behavior was the result of his insatiable sexual appetite. It's trite to say that men think with our dicks, but it's been scientifically proven that there's not enough blood to both the brain and penis to operate both simultaneously. Therefore, "Dick Logic" is actually the product of irrational behavior expressed through a man's penis that travels to his cerebrum. Men aren't insensitive, crude, non-committed, insecure, sick, twisted and misguided perverts. We just act this way because our penis tells us to.

Any women who says they met the man of their dreams need only live with him and they'll discover the wonder of "Dick Logic." A dick's not a trustworthy organ; it lacks a moral compass and craves variety. Dick Logic is also an equal opportunity destroyer contaminating the rich, poor, young, old, ethnic groups, religions and everything in between. The damage it causes is like a tsunami.

When a woman does something dreadful, she's considered "hormonal" because she did some bat shit crazy thing like shoot the family pet. However, women are absurd only once a month while men do outlandish shit thinking with our dick 24/7 three hundred and sixty five days a year. It's a testosterone thing, I'm told. A thinking dick has caused a President's impeachment, sullied hundreds of athlete's, embarrassed numerous celebrities, destroyed countless marriages and disgraced politicians (which, when you think about it, is actually an oxymoron for legislators).

You know you're growing up when you stop asking where you came from and refuse to tell your parents where you're going. It happens when you least expect it. One night, a little boy goes to bed entertaining thoughts that girls are gross, dinosaurs are cool and thinks about little league practice. The following morning, "Dick Logic" emerges and he wakes to hear another voice in his room (coming from his penis) proclaiming it has anointed itself Deity, Ayatollah and Master of his domain. From that moment on, it becomes his most prized possession.

Occasionally, accidents occur where a man's penis is severed, but you never hear of a guy accidentally cutting off his own dick. If that happens, you can bet the ranch a woman's involved (just ask John Wayne Bobbitt). Or proverbial severing occurs. For example, in 1968, the biggest Dick of them all (Richard Nixon) had campaign buttons made which read, "You can't lick Dick." After considerable deliberation, his advisers decided to destroy them because they realized they'd lose the women's vote. (Besides, what woman in their right mind would want to lick Milhous' penis except Pat?)

Rarely does an election cycle pass without some sanctimonious, evangelical, church-going, dick-head politician stand behind a podium confessing "Bumping Uglies" with a woman who didn't share his same last name. It happens so often that you'd think K Street would have lobbyists to offer Dick Logic damage control. These hypocritical scumbags classically feign grief, take responsibility for their actions and beg for forgiveness. Well, hello! Who else should bear your duplicitous shameful morality? You fucked up big time buddy and there's no Black guy to blame for this one. You douche bag, you're on your own.

The reason women aren't found in these compromising situations is simple. They've had to work extremely hard to attain their status and are less willing to risk everything for a roll in the hay. Others suggest that women are less susceptible to temptation because they're thinking with only one brain. Or maybe it's just that women are too damn busy doing their jobs and taking care of their families.

Dick Logic has happened ever since the beginning of time. The Bible cited Abraham and Jacob as adulterous husbands. The Romans had Caligula. Henry the VIII had six wives. In America, Thomas Jefferson thumped his concubine Sally Hemmings, which accounts for a whole lot Black folks named Jefferson. Warren Harding dipped his wick into at least two different women. FDR "dipsticked" Lucy Mercer (Eleanor's secretary). Everyone "liked Ike," including his personal driver Kay Summersby as Dwight "parked his Plymouth" in her furry garage.

JFK's amorous proclivities began long before he reached the Oval Office. He "boinked" White House staff, gangster's girlfriends, flight attendants, reporters, spies and movie stars. Who knows if any animals were ever involved? He "rocked the casbah" with Judith Exner (a former Sinatra babe) when she was "shtuping" Chicago mafia don Sam Giancana, who by the way was involved with Kennedy's assassination. When it was convenient, he "got busy" with Marilyn Monroe. His brother, Bobby, also did Marilyn.

Politicians really get around. Lyndon Johnson "drained his lizard" with Madeline Brown, resulting in an illegitimate son he financially supported. She alleged the affair lasted twenty years. Bush 41 "supposedly" buried "the one-eyed worm" with Jennifer Fitzgerald who served him in several different capacities (one was in the bedroom).

Gary Hart's presidential bid ended abruptly after an affair with Donna Rice was uncovered on a yacht named "Monkey Business." Barney Frank was reprimanded for a relationship with a male prostitute. Senator Bob Packwood resigned after ten women accused him of sexual harassment. Jim McGreevy stepped down as governor after disclosing an affair with another man. Governors Spitzer and Sanford as well as Senators Edwards, Ensign and Vitter were all caught "glazing their doughnuts" with women that weren't their wives. Even Martin Luther King "shook the sheets" with prostitutes the FBI discovered when they wire-tapped his hotel rooms and captured the sounds of sexual encounters.

And then there's "Slick Willie," the man who didn't inhale and redefined the definition of "is." He erected Dick Logic to an entirely new level. There was Jennifer, Paula and the Devil in the blue dress. Had the "slick one" evoked the "Dick Logic" defense, he might've skirted impeachment. Certainly some of his harshest critics would have been more forgiving since one of his enemies, Newt Gingrich, had two extramarital affairs — including one with his current wife that occurred during the time he was impeaching Clinton. Maybe we should forgive our public servants in spite of their indiscretions because after all, they're only as committed to anything as their options allow them.

Dick Logic is notably persistent among professional athletes. These guys deal with boredom of being on the road and women are attracted to them because of their status. Tiger Woods is the latest poster child for the time being. Although he's called Tiger, he's actually a cheetah. His lustful dick destroyed his squeaky-clean image forever. I guess you could say he wasn't on top of his game. Or maybe he was. He "hid the salami" with more women than Sleepy's has mattresses. On the front nine of his scandal were the women who came forward with allegations. When they asked Elin how many times she hit Tiger for his irresponsible behavior she replied: "I can't remember, just put me down for five."

Celebrities are famous for their kinky transgressions, but when half the women on the planet claim they were drugged and raped by Bill Cosby, I question Dr. Huxtable's wisdom. Why didn't he just pay for hookers? After all, he had the money. How niggardly of him to have been so foolish. If you wanted to enjoy her wares, all you had to do was pay her and follow her up the stairs.

Let's face reality, ladies. If you're looking for a sensitive, caring, great looking man, he's probably playing on the pink team. Women need a reason to consider sex, men merely have to find a place. It's basically a testosterone thing. When women are depressed, they eat or go shopping but Elaine Boozer noticed that men invade another country. It's a whole different way of thinking

Without the slightest provocation, men have erections and that validates their Dick's free will. Because our little head has but one eye it distinguishes women from an inverted perspective and concludes they all look the same. This assessment frequently ends with tragic consequences because sometimes you wake up the morning next to a woman so ugly they give Freddy Kruegger nightmares. These are the consequences when your little head does the thinking. There are several degrees of risk when "Dick Logic" is involved.

The first and most lethal after-effect is recognized as "jealous" DL. This is when the husband/ boyfriend catches another man in the act with his wife/girlfriend and pulls out a weapon in an insane jealous rage. You see it on the news all the time. "Tonight at 11: a man was found murdered on the South Side in what is thought to be 'jealous dick logic.' He was shot 27 times, fortunately three rounds missed. We'll have it all for you exclusively on channel six right after our completely asinine reality show you're watching. Stay tuned."

Next type of DL is the "deceptive" kind, where a married man's ring inexplicably disappears. He meets a woman who's searching for someone new and exciting. She has no clue she's being deceived and he doesn't fret because "captain winky" doesn't reason nor cares to. Compassion and Dick Logic are irreconcilable, which accounts for men cheating on their wives.

Men who cheat are never sorry about it unless or until they get caught.

The most distressing exercise of bad penis behavior is what's known as "delusional" DL. This occurs after several years of marriage as a guy echoes back on his accomplishments and concludes that he's an incredible person. He fancies himself as a successful, smart, funny and an absolutely incredible looking person! Yes, he's delusional. He's been an empty nester for several years and an afterthought to his wife in the bedroom. There's no sense putting lead in his pencil because the sex is boring, mechanical and rare. He's seen too many Viagra commercials and wants the Lion in his pocket to rear its ugly head once again. He considers trading in the old bag for a younger sexier model because he thinks he can afford it.

Many young women are attracted to these men (typically over 50) for an assortment of reasons. There's plenty of young women happy to marry them. Why? Because they understand it's worth having the entire pig because eventually they'll get a lot of his sausage.

Finally, Mr. Delusional pulls the trigger, leaves his wife and procures a trophy companion.

These beautiful looking creatures are very utilitarian. They function as lover, stepmother and a decorative ornament without having to use their brains. The end result is catastrophic for him, which can only be attributed to "his state of delusion." While he parades around with his new wife half his age to his male friends, the women remember his ex-wife who kept the family intact during his lucid years. Behind his back, the women smirk while the men ogle at his new toy's perky tits.

Meanwhile, the trophy babe is happy because she knows she's in it for the short term. The period of acting nursemaid, arm candy and perhaps bimbo is a temporary steppingstone to a better life. Call them "gold diggers" if you want, but these ladies have enough savvy to appreciate their peers are working at menial jobs living in tiny, shared apartments and several thousand dollars in debt with college loans. Mrs. Trophy understands she simply has to kiss some wrinkly ass and smile. Maybe she'll pop a Xanax and occasionally give him a roll in the hay with a secure future ahead. While he thinks his buddies envy him, she's thinking about not paying rent and in due course, when her friends will visit and party once he's gone. If he gets too talkative, she can hide his dentures. She'll party late because he's often snoring by ten. She knows he's with her for her looks and won't try to change her.

He'll always pick up the tab and sporadically have a few too many cocktails but doesn't have a drug addiction because his pot and coke days are behind him. Otherwise, he'd be on the other side of the dirt by now. She won't have to worry about him texting her because he doesn't know how. Her Hyundai sits in a garage because she's driving his Infiniti, Porsche, Lexus, Mercedes or BMW. He'll take her on fantastic vacations to Europe and Australia, ski trips to Aspen and Telluride and maybe an African safari.

After Mr. Delusion's dick calms down he realizes that sex is their only common denominator. He stops pretending that any meaningful relationship has a future when his record collection and favorite films and hers wouldn't even speak if they met at a party. (Steely Dan must have seen something when they wrote the lines, "Hey nineteen, that's Aretha Franklin, She don't remember, the Queen of soul, its hard time befallen, the soul survivors, she thinks I'm crazy, but I'm just growing old.) After his epiphany, he just wants to slip away quietly out the back door knowing his little head has ruined his life.

In the end, he explains the following to anyone still willing to listen. "After three years of marriage (my dick's name) and (insert her name here) have decided to part company. The decision is the result of much thought and consideration. My dick and (her name) remain wonderful caring friends with mutual admiration and respect for one another." Finally, he stares at his crotch and asks, "What the fuck were you thinking?"

There's a scene from the movie "When Harry Met Sally" that perfectly illustrates the dick's thought process.

Harry: "You realize of course that we could never be friends."

Sally: "Why not?"

Harry: "What I'm saying is -- and this is not a come-on in any way, shape or form -- is that men and women can't be friends because the sex part always gets in the way."

Sally: "That's not true. I have a number of men friends and there is no sex involved."

Harry: "No, you don't."

Sally: "Yes, I do."

Harry: "No, you don't."

Sally: "Yes, I do."

Harry: "You only think you do."

Sally: "You say I'm having sex with these men without my knowledge?"

Harry: "No, what I'm saying is they all WANT to have sex with you."

Sally: "They do not."

Harry: "Do too."

Sally: "They do not."

Sally: "How do you know?"

Harry: "Because, no man can be friends with a woman that he finds attractive, he always wants to have sex with her."

Sally: "So, you're saying that a man can be friends with a woman he finds unattractive?"

Harry: "No. You pretty much want to nail them, too."

What the movie illustrates is how men think. Ladies, here's a reality check: men are irrational beings with two brains residing in the same body. We can't fathom menstruation and you'll never understand Dick Logic. Let's call it a draw.

Did you ever wonder why men name their junk? The only similar comparison would be you naming your tits, which some ladies do. Of course, this a modest contrast because of the different attitudes each gender has about their privates. An article on pointsincase.com explains it as, "Men take pride in their member; they put it on a... pedestal, raising it above all else. You'll never hear a man complain about his cock, and you'll certainly never hear him criticize girls for staring at it. This is why men feel a need to name their junk." By doing so, they're personalizing what they love most, making something already special even closer.

The same article even goes on to say, "Not naming your penis is like forgetting to name one of your kids. Women will never understand it, and I don't expect them to." Branding your Dick personifies your character, which is why you really have think carefully before assigning it a name.

Back to my own life, now that I've tried to explain DL. I harken back to this one crazy night that provided insight as to what I should call my member. Should it be Troy, Hercules, Rocky, Russell the Muscle, Wilfred, Wendell, or Napoleon? So many names, only one dick.

I met this attractive-looking woman in a bar. We hit it off and left together. Back at her place, she showed me around and I notice her bedroom is jam-packed with teddy bears. There were small ones arranged along the floor, normal sized ones a shelf above. The next level contained gigantic bears. I was captivated by her magnificent collection. After we had a few drinks, we shared an intense night of sex. The next morning I rolled over and asked, "Well, how was it last night?" And she says, "You can have any prize from the bottom shelf."

That's why I named my dick Ozzie. It invokes feelings of an easygoing fuzzy Teddy Bear, and who doesn't like Koalas or Pandas? People adore teddy bears and take them into their arms. I loved Yogi and Boo-Boo as child. Bears are lovable and cuddly. The name Ozzie suggests one who's Open and Zany and Zestful who Ignites your passion and is extremely Enchanting.

If you ever meet a guy who doesn't nickname his "member," be very leery. He's probably on the same pink team with that caring sensitive guy. Not that there's anything wrong with that. It may just take you longer to find someone than you think. Before the existence of sexting, jerking off to internet porn and computer dating, men actually had to make an effort to find someone to be with. I searched the health clubs, supermarkets, parks, coffee houses and bookstores to meet women. No matter where I traveled, the easiest place to get lucky was visiting the local watering holes. Although bars are loud, congested and smoky, once the cocktails began a woman's inhibition vanishes and often their clothing disappeared as well by the end of the night. Depends on what you like.

Dicks don't discriminate, all though some have preferences. Some look for the Amazon with a perfect body and diva attitude, while others find humorous women more attractive. Some need women to take care of them. There are those who find mysterious women with a sense of independence appealing. Then, there are those who prefer the preppy type.

Being able to identify each category can increase your success rate and help you find what you're looking for. Women are all different. There are the cougars, ice queens, divorced women, society chicks, wing women, party girls and alcoholics just to reference a few that provoke a dick's longing. Some look rode hard and put away wet. But in the end, no matter the preference, they're easiest to find in bars.

Ozzie was always scheming ways to make sex happen. More times than I care to remember, I succumbed to his shenanigans. By the end of the evening, I'd contritely gaze down at my crotch and ask, "What the hell were you thinking?" He constantly hijacked my rational head.

One of Ozzie's favorite techniques was "the leave ugly early" principle. This strategy is based on the belief that guys (who aren't Tom Cruise, George Clooney or Brad Pitt) know the odds of leaving the cocktail palace with a stunning beauty are about the same as winning the lottery. By pursuing "visually challenged" females early, you skip "last call" when you're stuck with what's usually left of a bad lot of hideous looking women. The first thing in the human personality that dissolves in alcohol is dignity and by that time, drinking's given you the impression they're beautiful and you've wasted a fortune on booze you could've consumed at home with this Sasquatch for a lot less money. After all, when the lights are off, every woman's beautiful.

Happy Hour's the best time to consort with the opposite sex. The method of engagement depends on your ego. Women with average features are the easiest to approach because the pick-up artists usually start with the hottest babes then work the room until they've exhausted that group. According to Giovanni Casanova's "thirty rules when mixing adult beverages and trolling for women," Ozzie adheres to eight.

One: realize women are tricky, lying, manipulative, devious, scheming, sneaky, cunning, calculating, shrewd, and Machiavellian creatures, but love them anyway. We men are, after all, just rambling dicks.

Two: women communicate in two modes—the way things are and the way they WISH things were. When in doubt, assume it's the latter.

Three: women crave attention the way guys crave sex, so give concern sparingly; it's your currency.

Four: never forget there're plenty of women out there and stay away from the ones with more problems than you.

Five: never hit on any co-workers. Your job's taxing enough and if it doesn't work out, you've created a nightmare.

Six: Pay more attention to what women do than what they say.

Seven: remember that dating's a "numbers game" and accept you'll get rejected more times than not. Suck it up because even baseball hall of famer's only hit 300.

Eight: if you aren't sure about breaking a rule, go with your instinct. If it's wrong, it's a teaching moment and you'll know what to do the next time.

Of all my exploits pursuing women, the most disgraceful, appalling and despicable display of thinking with Ozzie occurred the night I met "Skylar." I was at my favorite bar one Friday night, when I noticed this breath taking raven-haired blue eyed sensation seated alone at the bar. She had the face of an angel with the body of a porn star. I didn't know if she was saving that seat for another; however, I scurried over to fill it.

While awaiting my beverage, I noticed her hand fingering the rim of her glass and sucking her middle digit into her mouth. Suddenly her head turned and our eyes engaged. With a certain "je ne sais quoi" I said, "You know you look like a decent conversationalist. My friends at the end of the bar bet me two hundred bucks I couldn't have a conversation with the most beautiful woman in this joint. How would you like to have a few cocktails at their expense?"

Astonishingly, that duplicitous line worked and she summoned the bartender, ordering a double Grey Goose "neat." Ozzie immediately recognized she was a woman to be taken seriously. She had my attention at neat. You could sense she was comfortable traveling solo. While accessible and receptive to a clever opening line, I knew she was the type who could just as quickly dismiss you. She knew she was special but I couldn't tell whether she was a person whose ego disqualified her looks.

Ladies who drink house booze are less discerning. They're just happy you bought them a cocktail. Women demanding pricey liquor are more exacting and believe they are entitled because they deem themselves special. They're opinionated, sophisticated, somewhat kinky and into gratification. They know they're hot and during the chase you don't get to decide if you can catch them—they do.

Her name was Skylar, but friends called her Sky. We began nestling cocktails, bantering back and forth and it turned out we shared a passion for golf. She was a five handicap and belonged to a local country club. I wasn't sure whether I was more captivated by her beauty or her handicap, which was seven strokes better than mine.

We swapped crooked stick stories and exchanged friendly glances as the noise in the bar grew increasing louder. Ozzie thought she was attainable and wanted to close the deal; however, this wouldn't be the first time he acted prematurely. At this point, I wasn't sure where this was going. I sensed Sky was enjoying herself and then seized the moment by inviting her to share dinner at a quieter venue around the block. She agreed to my proposal and we proceeded to our new destination. All the while I thought about the "leave ugly early" theory because tonight I was George Clooney.

We resumed our conversation at the restaurant and Skylar was a total delight. Not only was she visually arresting, she was beguiling as well. I exhausted my entire arsenal of "A" lines as the night wore on and was flattered that she had selected me. I knew she could have had the pick of the litter with any man with a pulse and (not on the pink team) at the other bar.

During dinner, I asked why she decided to dine with me. After a long pause, she leaned forward licked my ear and whispered I had a fascinating look. Once again, my ambiguous features camouflaged my genuine identity. Maybe I looked Greek that night. Who knows? But I was anxious to hear which box she'd check, so I asked what fascinating meant. She responded: "it's hard to say, but I'd guess that you're Italian." I replied: "That's a great guess; see I'm not that mysterious looking after all." She'd found her comfort zone and I was "Jiggy" with that.

Moments later, our romantic encounter took an astonishing turn for the worst. I asked her if one's ethnicity mattered if they found someone appealing. Her response was flabbergasting. Out of the lips of this beautiful looking person she replied, "Yeah, if they're niggers, gay guys or Jews."

Scare bleu! Murphy's Law time's a gazillion just occurred. In an instant, my night in Disneyland morphed into a visit to Auschwitz. Outside, this beautiful face harbored an internal derisive toxic mind. No matter how splendid she seemed, her bigoted beliefs compromised my entire value system. Just to see if I misheard her I asked what else she found offensive and her answers were equally repulsive.

I sat there silently dumbfounded, digesting her sentiments and knowing it was beyond me to associate with anyone fostering such repulsive values. Her beliefs were kryptonite as far as I was concerned. I quickly began to entertain ways to extricate myself from the evening as Ozzie began plotting how to get his way. "She wants to get laid! What are you thinking? She's keen on our company, inebriated and undoubtedly desires to have a meaningful one night stand."

Being the alcoholic I am, I ordered another vodka to reflect on the situation. Women know from the start just how far they're willing to invest their body knowing that they can always change their mind. At this point of the evening, our mutual attraction was apparent. I really didn't know what to do, but of course Ozzie did.

As we departed the restaurant, Ozzie briefly got the better of me as I embraced Skylar and gave her a passionate French kiss that appeared to catch her by surprise, but also take her breath away. When our lips unlocked, she moaned and rotated her hips against me and said "What will you do with me now?" Our eyes engaged and she invited me back to her place for a supposed nightcap. The sexual tension was reviving as the cocktails were taking their toll. The million dollar question was which brain would prevail?

A so called innocent nightcap morphed into two badly behaved people with dirty minds engaging in sizzling hot sex. Several times she offered her honor and each time I honored her offer as we satisfied ourselves into the wee hours. When the night evaporated, I woke up snuggled next to Sky's naked body and I realized the Oz man had won. I couldn't decide if it was more troubling that he compromised my entire value system or my coherent brain surrendered to the one eyed monster once again.

Nevertheless, Ozzie didn't care because he has no conscience.

Skylar woke shortly thereafter and we exchanged a morning kiss and good-humored small talk and fucked again. When it was over, I got up dressed and prepared to leave when she asked if we'd see each other again. I said, "Would you like to?"

Then she gazed at me with her enormous blue eyes and said, "That would be great. I had a delicious time last night. Why don't we catch eighteen at my club and I'll treat you to dinner next week." She jotted down her number and I sheepishly took her note. We embraced again and our lips locked passionately as she fondled my crotch while crossing the threshold.

Once outside, I slithered into my convertible, lit up a smoke and began assessing the previous evening. We met, had dinner and shared sex. We were strangers who lusted after each other. What she said during this exchange made me not to want to see her again. Has that happened before? A few of times. Did it last night? Clearly so. Sometimes people are beautiful; however, their loveliness doesn't make them noble. There's no beauty in bigotry. No honor in hate and no growth without acceptance. While driving away, I looked down at my pants shaking my head in disgust and asked Ozzie, "What the hell were you thinking?" His answer was obvious: Dick Logic! I flicked my smoke out on the road along with Sky's number and we never saw each other again. Whoever said one-night stands were supposed to be simple with no strings attached have clearly never met Ozzie. Because when you think with your Dick, persistence wears down resistance.

8

STINK'IN THINK'IN

*Sometimes a man wants to be stupid if it
lets him do a thing his cleverness forbids.*
— John Steinbeck

I consider myself middle-aged, but in truth I'd have to live to
130 to make that happen. In reality it's not how old you are,
it's how you're old. George Burns was telling jokes when he was
ninety nine. George Bush Sr. went skydiving on his ninetieth
birthday. Nelson Mandela was 76 when he became president.
Age is merely a mental construct.

I try to live in the moment and value the days I can still
remember. John Irving wrote in A Prayer for Owen Meany,
"Your memory is a monster; you forget—it doesn't. It simply
files things away. It keeps things for you or hides things from
you—and summons them to your recall with will of its own.
You think you have a memory, but it has you!" God, grant me
the senility to forget the people I never liked anyway, the good
fortune to run into the ones I do, and the eyesight to tell the
difference.

Of the six plus decades I've endured, the 1980's would be
the one I'd most likely never want to recall. It was jam-packed

with humiliation, remorse, guilt and was the nadir period of my life. It was a time when I was tormented with angst and self-doubt. I was marginally prosperous, yet not convinced if I was happy.

American culture changed forever as MTV turned the sounds of the music into the spectacle of vision. Music videos led us to the point where consumers stop listening to the message and started to buy what they saw. It was the beginning of what we call "optics" today. Video killed the radio star as new wave hit America from "across the pond." Cable TV tiptoed into our living rooms. Hair bands were the vogue, disco lost its glitter as hip-hop found an audience and people began break dancing. White kids imitated rappers as Black schools endorsed Ebonics.

Halfway around the world, the Iraqi's poisoned Iranians with chemicals we provided them. It was also a time when we were pals with Saddam Hussein. Apparently he did something to piss us off. Just ask Cheney, Rumsfeld and Bush about that. Between there and here, East Berliners pulverized a wall separating them from West Germany, ending the cold war. Both the Pope and President Reagan were shot. We lost John Lennon but discovered Madonna, Springsteen and Prince while Michael Jackson was still Black and donned one white glove singing "Beat It."

I was 30 when the decade began. I was no longer a teacher, but now employed as Account Executive at the radio station where my friend Murray previously worked. At the time, my complexion was more important than my qualifications and I fit their politically correct agenda, so they hired me.

I had traded my jeans and laid back attitude for expensive suits and an inflated ego. The station was infested with an excess of pompous slick people who made too much money and obeyed the rules decadently. I knew I was full of shit, but these people elevated crap to an entirely higher level. <u>They lived life upside down because they talked out their ass and the only thing that came out of their mouths was shit.</u> They got away with endorsing ad campaigns by marketing the station as new and approved. Now let me say this: if something is new, it couldn't be improved. Conversely, if something is improved, it can't be new. Somehow, these cheesy promotions worked.

Selling media advertising is analogous to statistical bigotry, matching age groups of male and females to advertisers who covet their spending power. Since I knew my fair share of bigots, this seemed like the perfect job for me. We worked very hard and partied even hardier. At that time, the radio business was a recipe of promotions, concerts, eccentric musicians, narcissism and of course sex, drugs and rock and roll. It was also an opportunity to hang out with the phony baloney "beautiful people." You almost thought you were important just by osmosis. Not everything about them was pretentious, but the majority of times they were.

After a few years I wore out my welcome and the station decided to replace me with someone whose shit they liked better. In the radio industry, people moved from station to station like dogs piss on trees. Every new regime brings in their own team. Even though I thought I had the jive, I really didn't fit in that world. However, I'm grateful to have had the ego-inflating experience. If at first you don't succeed, then maybe you just suck. Oh well.

Next I worked for a publishing company selling children's books to libraries and school systems. Several days a week, I'd pack my little TR7 with hundreds of books and meander throughout the state, engaging blue haired librarians who'd worked there since the Harding administration.

No matter what you're vending, you're actually selling yourself and I was good at that. But I grew weary of being confined in a child's world, talking about fictional characters. The Russians had just shot down a Korean airliner and the US embassy in Beirut had recently been bombed. I desired more reality and grew restless with the daily travel, so I decided to bid adieu to the wonderful world of children's books.

Things happen for a reason but sometimes the reason is because you're stupid. Leaving that job was truly a poor decision because I had nothing to replace it. Bills needed to be payed and everywhere I looked no one was willing to provide me work on my terms.

As my unemployment continued, the solution to my problems increased. I was running out of money. Suddenly, I had an epiphany: I'd deal drugs! Why should the government decide whose drugs were legal? They sanctioned the CIA to traffic cocaine out of South America so why shouldn't I sanction myself to deal coke, too? With that convoluted logic, I felt warranted to make a living selling drugs. Like all dealers, I sampled my product. Generally, I used coke as enticement to women to get laid. I preferred drinking, but lots of the ladies preferred coke because of its euphoric high during sex. I met quite a few women who spoke several languages, but few could say "no" in any of them once they did cocaine. They were coke whores, but nice ones, of course. They preferred not to listen to First Lady Nancy.

Although dealing wasn't the most prudent thing to do, the money was good and the demand was overwhelming so I didn't have to chase business; it pursued me. I had enough friends to establish a substantial clientele. I never did business with anyone I hadn't known for at least five years. I never keep drugs in my car other than when I needed to meet a customer. I never talked about any transaction over the phone and didn't ask anyone to help solicit business. My mantra was, "pigs get fat, but hogs get slaughtered."

Because of my healthy customer base, I wasn't actively pursuing legitimate employment. However, with several hours of down time, I explored legitimate ways to make a living from the profits I accrued. Eventually, this led me to another venture. In 1982, AT&T surrendered control of the Bell Operating Companies, which until then provided local telephone service in the United States. It now became possible for anyone to sell pay phones to businesses and customers who wanted to purchase them. So, I decided I'd invest in pay telephones.

For anyone born after 1980, there was once a world without smart phones and the countless apps we take for granted today. Believe it or not, people actually communicated by talking on telephones that were tethered to a wall. You were only as mobile as far as your cord stretched. In cases where you left the house, you used pay phones that were attached to phone booths requiring money to use them.

At first, I wasn't impressed by these new phones because they hadn't straightened out all the quirks. Then it dawned on me that in spite of their defects, that bars, restaurants and gas stations would need a booth to house their phone. I located a company that could manufacture phone booths and just like that I was in the telephone booth business.

Subsequently, I began placing ads in industry periodicals to solicit business. My new endeavor provided an opportunity to legally conceal my other enterprise. Now I was on top of the world and living the good life. Little did I know that my short lived success would all come thundering down and disaster would follow.

While attending a telephone convention in New Orleans, I received a call from a friend notifying me that my former girlfriend, "Mikie," had just been arrested for distributing an illegal controlled substance. As I listened to his words, my face turned ash white. That wasn't just any ordinary controlled substance—it was a controlled substance she acquired from me! A million thoughts raced through my head and none of them were good. How was she holding up? What did she say? Was there anyone there to post bail? Did she find a lawyer? Were they on to me? How did they catch her? What was I looking forward to back home?

I bolted from the convention and caught the next flight to Cleveland. You can bet your grannies panties that I was scared shitless. Of all the people in the world I never could have imagined, she'd be the person having me fitted for an orange jump suit. I was overwhelmed with thoughts of becoming the "Black is the new orange." I trusted her more than virtually anyone I knew. So much for the five year rule.

Mikie was my first true love and the only woman with whom I'd honestly shared my soul. Our liaison was the Montague and Capulet variety because she elected to live with me in spite of her parent's rejection as a result of our relationship. Blacks and Italians have traditionally had toxic racial problems in Cleveland. There were certain unspoken tenets recognized between both parties.

For instance, Black people knew to stay out of "Little Italy" or possibly suffer bodily harm. The mixing of the two were analogous to combining water with oil. They were the Dagos, Wops and Guido's to us; we were the niggers, jigaboos, jungle bunnies and porch monkeys to them. The only other word that starts with an "N" Italians could have used for Black people was neighbor, and that wasn't going to happen.

Her parents lived in an entirely White community where the only Black people they saw were the ones collecting their garbage. Mikie's high school was "pearly" white. Her parents felt humiliated when she told them she was sharing a house with (in their minds) a "Jigaboo." Instead of being curious that she could have feelings for someone that wasn't Italian never occurred to them. On general principle, they decided to dismiss her. My God, what would their relatives think?

While we were together, I'd never met her parents because they declined to visit. Probably the only more disturbing idea to them was if she dated a Jew! Although when you think about it, our situation was worse. The Jew could have been a doctor and possibly that might have been kosher with them. The irony was that because of my olive skin color I'm often mistaken as Italian. Countless times, I went to Little Italy and never experienced a problem. They just presumed I was a "Goombah" because they knew Black people understood the rules.

There was an animal magnetism between Mikie and me from the moment we met. We constantly had "monkey sex" as young lovers tend to do. Eventually, that ran its course and we acknowledged our physical connection wasn't meant for the long haul, yet we truly loved each other as people. And once we removed the sex from the equation, our relationship blossomed into a kindred bond and true friendship. We pledged to always have each other's back, no matter what. Most good friends will help you move into your new place, but she was the kind of friend who'd help you move a body. She was that special person who was wrong for me in just the right way. Although she was responsible for her own actions, she could've given me up to save herself. She didn't.

At the time, she was having an affair with one of the major stars on the Cleveland Browns. The cops thought she was his drug source. They assumed by catching her they'd get to him and he'd flip a few of his teammates to save himself. The narcs would then advance their careers with such a headline grabbing bust. They forcefully leaned on her hoping to get to him. In reality, this whole situation began because Mikie was strapped for cash and needed to make a few bucks to make ends meet.

She was in between jobs and had bills to pay. As one of my best friends and thinking nothing of it, I provided her with what she needed as a favor.

After all, I'd known Mikie for a dozen years and assumed she knew what she was doing. I actually dropped her off and waited in the car while she transacted her business. Upon returning, she handed me the money. I looked at the cash and immediately became suspicious because the bills were in sequential order. Nobody pays for dope like that except the cops. We instantly got the hell out of there and I told her that I needed to wash this money before I could compensate her. Little did I know, the cops thought I was the football star they were pursuing? Thank God we didn't get busted right then.

When the trial began, I was conspicuously absent for obvious reasons; however, I generously donated financially for her defense. She hired a prominent attorney who was an associate of one of my close friends, who was also a celebrated trial lawyer. We regularly partied and frequently hung out in clubs chasing women after hours. He was also good friends with Mikie. Because of these mitigating circumstances, he remained behind the scenes doing the leg work for his partner.

After both sides "picked twelve" and the trial was underway, I'd get daily briefings of the day's proceedings. She cooperated with the prosecutors as best she could, but never gave any names. I honestly thought she'd get off because they just couldn't turn her to catch their coveted prize. Essentially, the prosecution was unsuccessful in their quest to flip her and didn't get "Mr. Big." As a result, she was vindictively convicted and sentenced for two to ten years at a women's correctional facility in Central Ohio.

Once I was informed of the verdict, I sat alone in my office crying. I opened a large bottle of vodka and slowly sipped its contents until I medicated myself into an inconsolable mess, right along the lines of Dying Bites. "I got a bad case of the 3:00 am guilt's, you know when you're in bed awake and replay all those things you didn't do right? Because, as we all know nothing solves insomnia like a nice warm glass of regret, depression and self-loathing."

As the days passed, I became overcome with remorse. Here I was innocently sitting at home still dealing dope and Mikie was about to be confined and caged like an animal in the zoo. That thought looped through my mind like a vinyl record stuck in a groove. My drinking began increasing significantly, as F. Scott Fitzgerald must have known when he wrote, "Here's to alcohol, the rose colored glasses of life." Unexpectedly, her tragedy led to a relationship between me and her parents. Mikie's incarceration date was delayed for several months during which she stayed at home with her folks. I became a frequent visitor. During the day, she attended AA meetings to maintain her sobriety until she left for prison. After a while, her parents recognized that my bond with their daughter was indeed something special.

Mikie and I both had to a laugh when she mentioned that her parents were startled when I first came to visit because they thought I looked Italian. Imagine that? They were also pleased with my sizable contribution for her defense. We shared several meals together and gradually they began seeing me as a person and not a label.

The day before her incarceration, a few of Mikie's closest friends were invited to share her last day of freedom. It was the most somber and poignant time I'd experienced since I had laid my mom to rest a few years earlier. She and I cried intensely. My grief was as heavy as my guilt. I felt a vacuum in my soul. When you lose someone you love, you begin reassessing your life.

About six weeks later, I had a chance to visit Mikie at the correctional facility. She was allowed two non-family visitors per month and I always made the list. For two years, I'd make the hour and half commute each way to share an afternoon with her. I'll never forget my first visit. She was now living in gated community, though not the one she ever could have imagined. Approaching the institution, I couldn't help but notice how austere the buildings appeared with healthy landscaping of barbed wire and guards patrolling the outside.

Once inside, they performed a complete body search that more times than not gave the female guards a chance to cop a feel of Ozzie because they could. After that delightful experience, I was escorted to a table in the visiting area to wait for Mikie to arrive. We were permitted a brief embrace under the watchful eye of several guards. Then we'd sit down and catch up on local gossip as well as her horrific survival stories in prison. I'd always bring as much money permissible to put into her account.

The visiting area was about the size of a small high school cafeteria, accommodating maybe seventy-five people. There were a dozen or so vending machines adorning the wall and I always carried several rolls of quarters to satisfy whatever Mikie wanted to eat. The machines were a real treat for her because the prison food wasn't exactly epicurean.

I recall checking out the inmates scattered throughout the room and caught the eye of this hot looking prisoner. Call me a stupid chauvinist dickhead, but for whatever reason I never imagined eye-catching women (other than Mikie) who went to prison—probably because I never associated good looking people with nefarious intentions. I pointed the woman out to Mikie and asked why she was incarcerated and she began laughing hysterically. I couldn't imagine what was so amusing until she replied, "Honey, I don't think she's your type; she stabbed her husband twenty-five times. That's why her nickname is "Blade." The great thing about Mikie was that she was familiar with "dick logic" as a result of our living together. She said it was good to know that I was still thinking with Ozzie's brain, which we both found amusing.

That brief moment of levity softened the nightmare she was living daily. Her world revolved around routine, boredom and control. Her days weren't really days; they were just annoying obstacles that need to be faced. The times she was allowed visitors were the equivalent to being a child opening presents on Christmas. My visits lit up her spirits and seeing her was the only thing I looked forward to each month.

Covering the walls in the visiting area were murals depicting the various seasons of the year. For a few bucks, they'd take our picture as a keepsake of our encounter. Great keepsake! Over time, I'd collected all four seasons. The most difficult part of each visit was when it was time to leave. We always parted with grins and weepy eyes. The ride home was eternally depressing because no matter what I did, there was no way to alter her plight. My grief wasn't sorrow or tears. It was an overwhelming sense of numbness. In the wide, wide world of life, I was stuck in the agony of defeat.

The upside was that I had an exceptional therapist (vodka) which I visited frequently. Alcohol was the cause and solution to all my problems. I only drank on days beginning with "T"-Tuesdays, Thursdays, Today, and Tomorrow. It's pathetic the excuses I used to justify my consumption. (It's not drinking alone if your dog is with you.) After all, alcohol was legal and I wasn't hurting anyone. I could stop whenever I wanted. I knew I was "OK" to drive after drinking. "One more drink won't hurt." "It's what I do to make myself happy."

At first, I measured my drinking by having my first drink at five pm. That seemed to be rational because that's when happy hour begins. After a while, I began to incorporate time zones when I wanted to activate happy hour, which begins the slippery slope, again well-known to Fitzgerald. "First you take a drink, then the drink takes a drink, then the drink takes you." Where's the Bottom? They didn't make a glass big enough for me to have just one cocktail. An alcoholic is not a guy who thinks he's had one too many. He's usually the guy who thinks he's had one too few.

In spite of getting a DUI, I was in steadfast denial. Many of us drunks go years disavowing we're on a downward spiral. We need to reach a "bottom," the place where even the hardest of the hardcore drinkers finally admits their lives have become unmanageable. Being a "little bit alcoholic" is like being a "little bit pregnant." If you think you're an alcoholic, chances are, you are. I'd drink and have blackouts with no recall of the night before, trusting that my friends would refresh my memory. I often woke up in a blank space trying to recall how the evening disappeared. Sometimes there'd be an unexplained new bruise on my body. Other times, I'd find panties in my bed minus the woman I'd had sex with the night before. The worst nightmare was finding an empty barbecue box in the kitchen confirming a late night trip to the rib joint to modify my drunken stupor. Hello darkness my old friend, last night I visited you again.

One evening while out prospecting women, I spotted this alluring redhead and I immediately began to shadow her. We danced several times. When after cocktails, a few Quaaludes and meandering chit chat, we all of a sudden realized we had a previous encounter. No wonder the routine seemed so familiar. She was one of the mysterious missing panties from the past.

The sex was probably hot and nasty, but of course I can't remember. We had already had our meaningful one night stand. What's the point? We were both so fucked up during the first encounter it was blackout sex. If you want an instant asshole, just add alcohol. There are basically two levels of intoxication for most people: drunk and blackout drunk. We were the latter. They say alcoholism doesn't come in bottles, it comes in people. The excitement of tonight's conquest was suddenly diminished by the past.

To the sounds of "Last Dance," we kissed each other respectfully on the cheek and parted in different directions into the night. Remarkably, we would cross paths yet again only the next time, it was in a church basement reciting the Serenity prayer, drinking coffee and eating doughnuts. To paraphrase Bob Seger, "Ain't it funny how the night moves, when it seems you just don't have too much to lose, fucked up on drinks and one too many 'ludes?"

Ultimately, drinking became an excuse for doing nothing. I could easily see what was wrong with everyone else but myself. I pointed fingers at others, not realizing (as the people in AA like to say) three were pointing back at me. I was miserable and salvation wasn't in a bottle. I had no take on of living in the moment or a day at a time. I massaged my misery by drinking until fear gripped me. If I didn't change, nothing would change for me. The lucky ones find their bottom and reluctantly I was reaching mine.

I stopped dealing because I couldn't stomach the idea of surviving on coke money while Mikie lingered in prison. I was also paranoid the police were on to me. My phone booth business began to curtail as the months wore on. The new phones were riddled with glitches and weren't selling, which meant my booths weren't either. Soon money became tight. In time, I was missing mortgage payments and the credit card companies began calling. I was barely paying the utilities and my house was about to be foreclosed. Life was becoming unmanageable and I finally conceded that alcohol might be the problem.

The next time I visited Mikie we discussed my problem and she suggested I attend an AA meeting. She was now two years sober and her survival was encircled by AA. On the drive home that day, I decided to explore the idea of attending one of the meetings she suggested. What did I have to lose? After all, nothing's so bad that a drink won't make worse and I was at the point that I couldn't afford to drink.

It turned out there was a church that held AA meetings within spitting distance of my house. That next evening, I walked to the facility having no clue what was about to happen next. I wondered if I'd see anyone I knew. God forbid someone I knew learned I had a drinking problem. I thought I was perfect. As I crossed the threshold into the building, I noticed gaggles of women in attendance and Ozzie sensed we were on to something. There appeared to be no official hierarchy but apparently someone was in control. Various people orchestrated the proceedings.

I sat down processing the scene and noted the audience wasn't at all what I expected alcoholics to look like. I imagined them to be slovenly dressed men and women who looked weathered in appearance. This was not the case at all. Most of the audience was nattily attired and appeared to look normal. In fact, they looked like me. Imagine that? There were array of people of different ages, races and faiths. The meeting began with the Serenity Prayer and everyone stood up and recited it as I mumbled along not knowing the words. "God grant me the serenity to accept the things I cannot change; courage to change the things I can; and wisdom to know the difference." That sounded OK to me so far. Then I sat there and listened to someone tell their account about how they became an alcoholic. Their story was interesting because it seemed similar to mine. Afterwards, those who chose to comment did so. Nobody was required to speak and no one took issue with what that person said because it was politically incorrect to "take someone else's inventory." I guess it's hard for

one drunk to criticize another. After all it takes two to lie...
One to lie and one to listen.

After the comments, they asked if anyone was attending
their first AA meeting was willing to acknowledge themselves
by standing up. This became my moment of truth. I was in
a room with self-confessed drunks. Did I have the courage
to admit I was member of their club? Was I really a prisoner
to vodka? Had I been deluding myself for all these years? I
stood up, admitting I was an alcoholic to a group of strangers
(which gave me an adrenaline rush). The audience applauded
to congratulate me for the courage to admit that my life was
just as fucked up as theirs.

As the meeting adjourned, several people invited me to
join them for coffee. I was told several times that the program
doesn't fail; you fail if you lie to yourself—just fake it until
you make it. Days became weeks and weeks turned to month's
visiting schools, temples and church basements hearing how
people negotiated life without a drink. I eventually got a
sponsor to mentor me in case I entertained thoughts about
falling off the wagon.

I was about a year into AA when Mikie was released
from prison. It took her a while to adapt to her unrestricted
environment after being confined for so long. I'd attend
meetings where she told her story that usually brought down
the house. People requested her to share her story wherever we
went. She was celebrated in the Program.

I wish I could say it was entirely my misery and desire for a
new life that kept me coming back to those basements, but that
would only be somewhat true. My allegiance to the program
could also be attributed to "Dick Logic." When women waxed
poetic accounts of their desperation, many times I'd listen
attentively while thinking about getting into their pants. Here,
are all these women and there's no sexual lubricant other than

the Program. The sex often times replaced the booze. Amy Dresner sums it up well in Sex and Dating in Sobriety.

Dating in AA is similar to hooking up in a fish tank. There's a limited supply of people and we recycle each other. It's fishing in a miniature toxic pond. And you'll often hear sayings, like, "Odds are good that you'll meet somebody, but the goods are odd."

I tried to be discreet attending meetings out my area, but even if you drive and hour and go to "bumfuck" where nobody knows you, word gets out. Eventually, a secret's worth hinges on the people from whom it must be kept and people in AA try hard to be honest. It was only a matter of time before everyone knew what I was doing and Dresner lays it clear. "The 'grapevine' couldn't be a better metaphor for the growing gossip and intertwining overgrowth that is the fellowship of AA. And let us not forget about the amends that have to be exchanged once the relationship has gone awry."

After living sober for a few years, my Program gradually began to deteriorate. I'd engaged a number of women from various meetings and the monotony of talking the "steps" got old, so out of boredom, I began going to bars. It's astonishing how their drinking mysteriously enhanced my appearance. I'd nurse a couple of ginger ales with lime and as the night wore on, I was meeting ladies who barely noticed me earlier. I was their best of a bad lot of men. Ozzie was elated just to have some exercise. I liberally tipped the bartenders because they're the ones who helps drunk people get laid. All the while, I remained sober and continued attending meetings.

Sporadically, I'd be asked to tell my story and lead a meeting. On those occasions, I'd bring Mikie because she was my ace in the hole. After honestly explaining how I stayed sober, inevitably people took exception to my behavior. Their general consensus was that I wasn't practicing "The Program" correctly. One of the million bumper sticker slogans in AA is "Dry people and dry places." The fact that I frequented bars was tantamount to blasphemy. Of course, I didn't give a shit because Ozzie wasn't the alcoholic; I was.

After I was lambasted by their comments, Mikie the acknowledged "saint" of AA would stand up and remind them I stayed sober. It was working for me so what right did they have to "take my inventory." They were pointing fingers and you know what that means. But it took its toll. After five years of sobriety, I left the Program. Somewhere along the line, I began to figure out I didn't need meetings to improve my life. I've taken a lot away from those basements that have enhanced my life. I now have faith instead of despair, courage instead of fear and self-respect instead of self-contempt. Serenity isn't the absence of conflict, but the ability to cope with it. I'll always be an alcoholic; however, today I'm a practicing one who occasionally drinks at home with my wife.

Mikie eventually married someone from the Program and her mother asked me to accompany her down the aisle during the ceremony. When you consider how hard it is to change yourself, you understand what little chance you have trying to change others. Yet I changed and Mikie changed. Her mother and father changed their attitude about me and I changed my view of them. Einstein was right on the money when he noted, "the world as we have created it is a process of our thinking. It cannot be changed without changing our thinking."

9

MAC THE KNIFE

> *Better to put your heart on the line, risk everything, and walk away with nothing than play it safe. Love is a lot of things, but "safe" isn't one of them.*
> — **Mandy Hale**

Please respect old people. We graduated high school without Google and Wikipedia. We appreciate reality (though I'm not sure what is actual reality and what masquerades as truth). We've traded compassion for indifference and it's reduced our capacity to comprehend honestly. Reason and legitimacy have been usurped. No longer do we worry about children cutting school out of boredom; instead, we cringe at the thought they might be murdered by classmates who've watched video games that have desensitized them of the consequences of killing. It's startling how artificial life's become. People text each other to terminate relationships and take pictures of their genitals to begin one. It's unmitigated nonsense.

A shocking difference in today's world was noted by New York Times columnist Seth Davidowitz on September 20, 2015 in the Sunday Review:

In the era before digital data, there were debates about the relative popularity of celebrities and deities, most famously when John Lennon claimed that the Beatles were more popular than Jesus. Lennon didn't live long enough to compare Google search counts. Today, it is pretty clear that Jesus does not get the most attention, at least online. There are 4.7 million searches every year for Jesus Christ. The pope gets 2.95 million. There are 49 million for Kim Kardashian. This is hardly definitive proof that Kim Kardashian is more popular than Jesus or Pope Francis, or that this country now worships at the altar of the Kardashians, but the differences are nonetheless striking.

This drivel began in the 1990s, which was the last vestige of virtue. Keyboards were fixed to pianos, programs were seen on TV, a web was a spider's home, the flu was a virus that kept you from work and backup happened to your toilet. Memory was something lost with age and unzipping anything in public was considered lewd behavior. Newspapers were relevant and people purchased merchandise in "brick and mortar" buildings.

At the start of the decade, computers with balky screens began littering offices and cell phones the size of a football became available to consumers. People began defining work hours on their own terms. Millennials would be hard-pressed to grasp the '90s scene what with today's e-mailing, texting, tweeting, instant messaging and twittering their every thought. This was the last time you could actually get lost. Just ask D.B. Cooper. If you can find him.

We were years away before anyone knew the difference between Barack Hussein Obama and Osama Bin Laden. The significant political issues were healthcare, social security reform and gun control; which to this day are still unresolved and as contentious as ever. Only in America do we use the word 'politics' to describe the process so well: "poli" in Latin meaning 'many' and "tics" meaning 'bloodsucking creatures'. For those too young to have experienced the 90s, I assure you it was fun and forever gone like tears in the rain. Of course, back then I was thinner, better looking and wore a younger man's clothes.

I'd accrued four years of sobriety, emerged from bankruptcy and made a decent living selling cable TV advertising. No longer did I measure my success by my peers. I'd wasted the last decade on ploys to work the system and now I was working on myself. The ambiguity of life was fading. I'd lived through defeat, rallied from hardship and accepted living on life's terms because life's short (and they say begins at forty). But, so does bad eyesight and being asked to slow down by your doctor more than the police.

As much as my life had improved, matters with the opposite sex remained the same. My heart was unable to fasten itself to someone. Most men know what they hate but few are aware of what they love except sex, sports and a good meal. I was afraid of commitment because I feared my warts would be uncovered and I'd be dismissed. Rejection's a bitch. I hadn't reached the point to love myself enough to appreciate what it meant to love another. In my view, I agree with the tennis star Martina Navratilova. "The difference between 'involvement' and 'commitment' was like a ham and egg breakfast. The chicken was 'involved' – the pig was 'committed.'"

Not to switch gears and cause a parallel between chickens, pigs and women, I once dated a "fetching" woman from AA. We'd both attended similar meetings and eventually decided to hook up. The sex was good and she seemed to be normal. Then one evening as she drove away, I noticed a vanity plate which read "HOT-1" on her raggedy Dodge Dart. That seemed a little too pretentious and that's all it took to dismiss her. Everyone knows people who need attention the most advertise it on their license plates. (Besides, who puts vanity plates on a fuck'in Dodge Dart? You need a Mercedes or a Rolls to legitimize that kind of conceit.)

Most men dismiss women with similar typical lame excuses: "It's not you, it's me," or "I'm not looking to get serious," or "You deserve better," but all I needed was a license plate. When you perceive yourself as flawed, it's easy to find imperfections in others. After dating someone for brief periods, I'd look for just the slightest imperfection to thwart commitment issues. Of course, dating works both ways. Some women just didn't find me appealing. Not everyone's going to like your chili. I wore out relationships like women wear out panty hose. The instant I realized someone had nothing stimulating to offer (other than sex), I vanished. I guarded my feelings and was allergic to the phrase "till death do us part." Good women frightened me because they wanted my emotion, and what was left of mine, I didn't wanted to share.

Don't get me wrong, I believe marriage is a wonderful institution, I'm just averse to institutions. It all began with that "God" thing. Countless friends thought I should be committed, but it wasn't to matrimony—their idea had something to do with straightjackets. Several of my former wingmen married early, had kids and became responsible adults. From time to time, we'd hang out and many of them envied my independent status while their wives doubted if I'd ever grow up. I was content living solo. It had its benefits. I set up my place to my taste and never had to wait to use the bathroom. The only downside was that I had to troll to get laid. But living alone also meant you never got caught jerking off.

Roaming around to find people was different then. Socializing in the '90s was vastly different than it is today. I'm sure computer dating is great until you discover your date has been cutting and pasting their orgasms. Or even worse, when you find the object of your affection is a muscular, forty-five-year-old baldheaded dude, rather than the hot, twenty-five-year-old babe he pretended to be.

Back then, the rules of engagement required actual face to face discussion. You knew nothing about them because you couldn't Google, Facebook or background check (and that was part of the thrill). Most dalliances lasted as long as Ozzie was motivated and that depended on how long the other person decided to play. Ozzie agrees with Lisa Kleypas. "Dating is like trying to make a meal out of leftovers. Some leftovers actually get better when they've had a little time to mature. But others should be thrown out right away, No matter how you try to warm them up, they're never as good as when they were new".

Dancing was a big part of dating. Unfortunately, I inherited my mom's lame white rhythm instead of my dad's black dexterity. Let's put it this way: I was the "Vanilla Ice" of dancing. In spite of my marginal agility, I pretended as if nobody was watching. Anyway, who dances sober unless they can really dance?

And it didn't matter if I couldn't really dance to pick up women. There's a bar for every kind of person and a bar for every type of drink. They're are Sports Bars, Gay Bars, Wine Bars, Vodka bars, Cigar bars, Singles Bars and each has a different ambiance, but the same cast of characters. One of the best things about bars is also one of the worst: you never know who'll meet and there's plenty of people saloons could do without. They're the ones who ruin everything from ordering a drink, to destroying your entire evening.

People can make or break a place. There's that garish woman who's just a tad too aggressive, haunting the establishment like an assassin stalks its prey. She'll force you to dance, or hang nearby and marry herself into your conversation until you buy her a drink. If Ozzie was as big as her mouth, I might be interested. She's easy pickings and most men rarely refuse an opportunity. Just think of "Dick Logic" and the leave ugly early theory. Mickey Rourke must have known some of these women. "The only problem is that she's a broken down old beast rode hard and put away wet with a cigarette ravaged voice and smells like Sasquatch. At 2AM, with a few drinks in you, it might not seem so bad, but try to think about the next day, when your buddies are fuck'in with you for hooking up with a chick that looked like Chewbacca." I try to circumvent that, but at times Ozzie's gotten the better of me.

When I wasn't shaking my ass on the dance floor, I'd visit the personal ads. This proved adventurous to say the least. Since women don't come with written instructions, you did what you thought was most effective in order to catch their attention. You had to watch what you said because it might sound too sexist, arrogant or clichéd deeming you un-swoon-worthy.

A truthfully candid personal ad should read: I want a meaningful one night liaison but actually I prefer to date myself, only with more money; I'm emotionally insecure, on medication, passionate and a sloppy drunk but adventurous; I've slept with everyone and do a lot of pills and I've occasionally been called a bitch. However, you never got those kinds of ads.

Responding to the personals was a numbers game. There might be seventy five ads and after eliminating the ones that liked "long walks on the beach," Merlot, candlelight dinners and soulful conversation, you called the nine that were left. Of those who responded, they ended the conversation first because they wanted you to think their time was valuable. They'd only agree to dinner for Saturday if you called before Wednesday. Most dressed suggestively hoping you'd take notice. The very discerning women met for coffee before committing to dinner. They chose to maximize their time just in case you weren't their type or appeared to be a dick. For the initial rendezvous, you'd describe your outfit in order to find each other.

I'd usually wear something completely different and have my wingman page me ten minutes into each engagement. This provided an excuse to extricate myself from any horrible encounter. I always anticipated the worst because (unless they were recently widowed or rebounding from a recent break up), the "hot ones" were still grieving and off the dating circuit. Low expectations cushion the letdown of a bad match and were needed as a filter. One occasion, I arrived for a date and several women fit the general description. I assessed the situation and strolled over to the most unappealing woman, introduced myself and she was astounded I was able to spot her so quickly. That's why I had wingmen, pagers and low expectations. It is one thing to be underwhelmed and run away, but a true gentleman is always prepared.

Although I was secure being a bachelor, there were moments of anxiety living alone. We're born alone, die alone and in spite of our social collaborations, ultimately alone in our cerebral universe. For the most part, being alone was terrific but sometimes didn't feel quite right. Up to this point, I thought it was better to be unhappy alone than to be unhappy with someone else incompatible.

In reality, I had esprit de corps with someone who spoke few words and was the utmost wingman I'd ever known. His name was Winston and he was my chocolate Lab. We were a lot alike. We shared a fascination for women's crotches, both marked our territory and our bark was often much less threatening than our bite. He was my buddy, pal and faithful

companion. We were also akin because we w
trying to bury our bone somewhere.

His routine was simple. He lived to eat, pla
He never had any ulterior motives, didn't play mind game
or second-guess me unless it concerned food. Winston was
void of guilt, never carried a grudge and never criticized any
my friends. He was happy watching football, never wanted to
shop, didn't care if I left the toilet seat up, rarely complained
and did nothing for political reasons. The more women I dated,
the more I loved my dog. There's that old adage that men are
like dogs and cats are like women. To some extent, it's true.
Cats are manipulative, prodigal creatures that only want you
when they want you. Dogs are straightforward and honest
animals. A dog's efforts to gain your attention are frank, not a
subtle gauged seduction like a cat. I'd take Winston to the park
because he was a "chick magnet." Unfortunately, the women
ogled him and barely paid me notice. Winston wasn't my whole
life, but he made my life whole.

In retrospect, I deeply lament being so blasé about caring
for my friend. I channeled much of my behavior through
him. At times, he'd sneak out in the pursuit dogs in heat. He
always returned home either later that evening or early the next
morning. If not, I would bail him out at the dog pound. I knew
the warden on a first name basis. Occasionally, he'd call to let
me know that Winston had a sleep over. I'm sure he thought
I was a dickhead for being so remiss, but sometimes you don't
want to admit you're a jerk even if you are.

For whatever reasons, I thought nothing of the consequences
of my irresponsibility. Winston didn't care and loved me
unconditionally, which is more than I can say about any of the
women I shared time with. They say there's a lid for every pot,
yet I hadn't met someone to cover my container. There was no
right person, just various degrees of incompatible ones. They

ɹere either neurotic, moody, insecure, or demanding. Take your pick. I invariably selected the incongruous ones.

I likened my dating life to a Far Side cartoon that depicts Bob the spoon, Ernie the fork and Mac the knife. The caption reads: In the early days living in their squalid apartment, all three shared dreams of success. In the end, Bob the spoon and Ernie the fork ended in the old silverware drawer and only Mac the knife went on to fame and fortune. With that said, the utensils in my drawer of relationships have been stocked with Bob's spoons and Ernie's forks, but never that elusive knife named Mac.

The first fork I discovered was Nora. She was an Irish Lass with an extraordinary ass that any man could fancy. She drank like a guy, was terrifically funny, fucked like a bunny and did what she wanted to do on her terms. She was always out of place in just the right way. We were both alcoholics, only she wouldn't admit it. Not only was she an inappropriate match, she was someone I fell head over heels knowing it was a doomed romance from the beginning.

What enthralled me about this woman was her cavalier attitude never taking herself seriously. She had Ali McGraw looks with a smile that disarmed me. I was completely intoxicated by her because of the noxious component she added to my contaminated life. We were never meant for the long haul because obstacles existed that were beyond my control. The odds of us sharing an everlasting future were about the same as a Black guy joining the Aryan Nation.

I tempted her desires because of my swarthy look that contrasted the "yuppie" guys she'd previously dated. They were Wonder Bread and I was pumpernickel. Our relationship was conditional (at best) because her pedigree forbade serious consideration. Nora was country club minted, and mindful that daddy would never sanction our merger. To her, our relationship was merely a temporary dalliance. It was delusional to think there was a future in our affair, but I didn't care. Oscar Wilde once said, "The optimist sees the donut, the pessimist sees the hole." All I wanted to see was breakfast.

Ozzie was the realist. He didn't care and knew Nora and I liked the same bat crazy shit (for now, which didn't mean we had to be lifelong soul mates). His only attachment to anything was to my body. To him, people were meant to be used, not loved. Nora and I lasted a couple of years, until she saw that one person we'd all take back no matter how much they hurt us in the past. One of her previous flings was a friend of her family and fit in to that well-heeled network. He was the round peg to my square hole and she lived in the world of rounds pegs. And there you have it "Nah, Nah, Nah, hay, hay, hay—goodbye."

After Nora and I parted ways, I started dating black women. They were considered spoons to me because I preferred white women. I never intentionally avoided the colored ladies, it's just that they didn't orbit in my universe. They worried me because when things got somewhat serious, they'd take me to meet their parents.

It always amused me that when I'd bring a black girl to a party my white friends would say that she's a keeper. Was that because we were both black and therefore like-minded? They never said that when I dated blondes. Besides, who knew whether she wanted me to be her one? It was that kind of warped logic that reinforced my oath to non-conformity, sort of like Groucho Marx's maxim. "I don't want to belong to any club that will accept people like me as a member."

Dating people of different colors is an interesting exercise. It's difficult when you don't follow the cookie-cutter mold of what a relationship should look like. I've found it's more important to listen to my heart than pay attention to someone's pigment. People look at interracial couples through their own racial lens—and I don't care what they think. To me, laundry's the only thing that should be separated by color. However, I do perceive a difference in attitude between white women and black women.

For instance, how women react to certain attributes is telling. Self-deprecation is a certain side of my personality which white women find appealing. It defuses the "Angry Black Man" persona. Black women are completely opposite because they seek strong partners with jobs who aren't trying to evade the police. Lena Horne once said, "It's not the load that breaks you down, it's the way you carry it." Black women are wired to assume they'll rear children without help and have to work to manage the family. You rarely hear a black athlete thank their father during an interview because, in a lot of cases, he wasn't around.

Here's a prime example. Once I had a fling with a woman whose family owned a few Black funeral homes in Cleveland. They had a notable presence in the community in addition to considerable money. In Cleveland, they kill a lot of Black folks and there's only so many places to bury us—they buried their fair share. She and I got together (because I capitulated to Ozzie), and my first thought the next morning was this woman reminded me of an early version of Chewbacca. Every girl has the right to be ugly, but she abused the privilege. I had a dreadful hang over and all I can say is that drinking made her beautiful the night before.

When she awoke, she was delighted about the previous evening and asked me out for a date. I didn't want to appear as if she was a consolation prize (because drinking enhanced her appearance), so I agreed to see her again. As she was the heir to the family business and after a few encounters, it was obvious that she needed a husband to improve her standing in the family business.

It was also evident that daddy had given his approval. As much as I might have fancied marrying into real money, the thought of getting hitched to women who looked like a Star Wars character didn't settle well with me. Groucho's aphorism resonated loud and clear. It's not hard to figure out what you'll sacrifice in order to be happy and money doesn't guarantee happiness (although it does let you choose your own form of misery depending on your disposition not your circumstances). So much for that.

The next artificial relationship was with a Jewish girl. She was actually a Spork (a hybrid spoon and a fork). At the time, I was living downstairs in a duplex and Hila was minding her sister's pets upstairs. One evening, she knocked on my door to borrow something. After several minutes of pleasant banter, we were smoking pot and before you know it—naked and exchanging fluid. The next morning, we reflected on the previous evening.

Hila was a kosher Jew, but was uncommitted. In a lot of ways, we shared similar beliefs. Her kinky tenets jived with my peculiar views, so we began seeing each other on a regular basis. Around a year later, I bought a house and asked her to share it with me, which provided much consternation to her father. He was a very religious Jew and a pillar in the Jewish community... and somewhat critical of non-Hebrews (or as they say in Yiddish a "mocker").

The irony of our relationship was acutely opposite from the one I shared with Nora. Hila also fit in to the privileged class, except she had the chutzpah to follow her own convictions. Daddy just couldn't fathom how his daughter could live with a "schvartze." It just wasn't kosher. In his mind, he'd provided her with everything she ever wanted and she rewarded his largess by humiliating him. While she and I continued having a grand old time, her father anguished. Unbeknownst to Hila, her father offered me a considerable amount of money to dissolve our relationship.

I was both flattered and stunned by his generous proposal, but by and large offended that he thought money would put an end to his personal torment. After all, I could have married the funeral directors daughter and I walked away from that. His discontent and frustration was entirely his own creation.

She and I were serious about each other but I was troubled about and the money she'd leave behind as an outcast from her family. I think that's what frightened me the most. She was willing to walk away from her family for me. Although we were on the same page about money and happiness, there are two things I am not: a fraud or a home wrecker. I just couldn't be a wedge that divided a family.

Every now and then, relationships end not because they've failed but because you know they're not meant to be. If you're not sure it's right for you, it's probably not right for that someone else. I wasn't about to be a point of contention. Letting go didn't mean I didn't care about her anymore. I just wasn't willing to let her suffer in the future if our relationship didn't go the distance. For one of the few times in my life, I could honestly say, "It isn't about you; it's really about me." Once again, no knife.

One of the hardest things to do is to dismiss someone and you can't explain why. In the end, our choices define us and this was one I knew was right. I wanted to tell her about her father's offer but I couldn't. It just wasn't meant to be and our breakup was the right thing to do. So once again I'm flying solo and back to having pension sex. You know the kind where you get a little each month but not enough to live on.

Call me an asshole, but when you're dealing with Ozzie he knows when to go to the bullpen so back to AA we went. You might call him my personal Marino Rivera. That's when

I discovered another fork in the drawer. Her name was Leslie. She was several years my junior and the best gift she had to give was her the ability to receive. To fill a sexual void, I attached myself to her. The world's a really callous place surrounded by noxious people, and women in the program fall into the trap of having unhealthy relationships confusing romance with recovery.

Leslie and I met in a church basement over coffee at an AA meeting. The thing about AA is that it's similar to hooking up in prison. There's a restricted supply of broken people and we recycle each other. However attractive Leslie looked on the outside she was less so from within, but at least she was better than Skylar because she wasn't a bigot. She was a five foot ten blue-eyed blonde who was bright, attractive and aggressive. I should have suspected her needy demeanor when she dismissed Winston as merely a dog and not my faithful wingman. If she snubbed a creature that loved me more than I loved myself, it should've been obvious I was dealing with a selfish and high maintenance woman. Ignoring that was truly a foolish move.

She moved into my place and I quickly realized her blonde hair and never-ending legs couldn't substitute for maturity and compassion. As a general rule, time suggests wisdom, but bad Dick Logic negates that. She expected a concierge and I just wanted to share time and have sex. Successful relationships are about quid pro quo but she was generally taking and seldom giving.

Occasionally, we'd visit her parents and I sensed they were freaking out because I was living with their daughter. I was closer to their age. I had this eerie feeling I was her proxy-dad instead of her lover. She had an air of entitlement and was overly judgmental. Our only glue was sex and soon that became passive and perfunctory. Conversations became sporadic and gradually faded. We'd exhausted every reason to stay together and were destined to split up. But while we shared the same space, we began living separate social lives. She began searching for different accommodations and networked her support through AA. I took comfort taking out women at various clubs.

As a forty something bachelor, the notion of living the rest of my life alone was unsettling. Why hadn't I found that elusive knife? My happiness wasn't centered on being with someone else, but I was slowly becoming Al Green and tired of being alone. The idea of marrying was an elusive thought. It was time to step up my game and do something about it.

I started dating a variety of women. Of course Ozzie oversaw my choices and assessed who he preferred (which for the most part involved any breathing female). His guidelines were very generous but, then again, what did he know. Men generally grade women from one to ten because we rate everything. It could be the ten greatest football players, gangster movies, guitarists or cars. We don't exchange conversations about issues we talk about things.

Women share their feelings while men just talk bullshit. A guy can walk into any situation and start talking with another dude just by saying, "What'd you think about last night's game?" Thus begins our discussion. Debating women's aesthetic features is another by-product of our tendency to rate, measure and compete. The reasoning goes like this: the hotter a woman is — i.e., the higher on the 10-scale she is — the more often she's hit on and therefore harder to pick up. We base entire strategies and behaviors around a woman's appearance. The 10-scale is a benchmark for our own accomplishments. The physical appearance of women is used as a form of measurement.

It's all about bragging rights (a testosterone thing). If I said, "I hooked up with a ten last weekend," guys get a certain mental image in their mind, whether it's the tall blonde with big tits or the black girl with a fabulous ass. In either case, they're totally impressed because all guys have a vision of their ten. I'd say Leslie was about a seven and a half. She lost a few points because of her selfishness and indifference towards others.

Some search forever looking for that special other who leaves a footprint on your heart. You're complete opposites, yet that balances the union. In time, you realize they're honest, ethical and reliable. You can't hide your blemishes, so you don't try to. You'll clash occasionally but pardon each other because the depth of the relationship. You're willing to risk having your heart broken and don't ask the other to solve your own emotional issues. Being together doesn't require constant chit chat because you're content sharing the same universe in silence. This doesn't happen to everyone, but after all the spoons and forks I'd found in my drawer, I finally found Mac the knife.

10

BERNIE

*Love is just a word, until someone comes
along and gives it meaning.*
— Paulo Cohelo

I'm told there are five excuses for drinking: the first is for the
effect, the second to grieve, the third is to relieve stress, the
fourth for liberating inhibition and the fifth is for any other
reason you can think of. I chose the fifth and returned to
drinking again. I respect the power of addiction, but there's a
middle ground between drinking and death. AA got my life
back in order, but there's no "law" you have to remain loyal to
that regimen.

For a variety of reasons, AA wasn't the ultimate solution or
perfect answer for my recovery. Some need a 12-step program
and maintain a life around sober friends and activities, while I
used the program as a "bridge" back to life. I practiced staying
in the moment, honestly evaluating my inventory and drinking
responsibly (which to some may be an oxymoron). "Starkle,
starkle, little twink, who the hell I are you think? I not under
the alchofluence of inkahol, like some folks thank I all. I only
had tee martoonies!"

I reverted back to dating the same variety of utensils again - the sporks, forks, and spoons. You know what they say about doing the same thing over and over and expecting different results. And then, after a year or so of this insanity, serendipity occurred.

I was in a bar having a conversation with a colleague when in walked an attractive lady that quickly commanded my attention. She had flowing brown hair and a radiant smile with a killer figure. Ozzie thought she was at least an eight and perhaps higher, but I couldn't gauge that until we actually had a chance to meet. I decided to use obscure pickup line 99, which is intended for dog lovers. It's a risky move because she may favor cats or even worse not like animals at all. One thing I learned from the Leslie debacle was that no one was going treat Winston the way she did.

I eventually approached her and said: "I sense you're a person who loves dogs" and she enthusiastically said yes, completely validating line 99. Seeing that she had a thing for dogs, I instantly produced a picture of Winston. It turns out she'd owned a Dachshund named "Jasper" and we began trading dog stories.

Bernadine was her name but she preferred to be called Bernie. She'd recently been transferred from an east coast pharmaceutical company. Unrelenting travel prohibited her from having a pet. As a district manager, she was constantly on the road facilitating her sales staff in four states. As the evening evolved I championed the merits of Winston hoping she'd attribute his virtues to me. I wasn't certain whether that worked, but she did want to meet my dog.

Several beverages later, we parted company. I was impressed by her inner beauty as she expressed herself and I could sense she was comfortable being herself. She was truly a lovely person without flaunting it. Could she possibly be that elusive knife?

By chance, we reunited weeks later at a different watering hole and she immediately asked about Winston. I was impressed she'd remembered his name and again I championed him, hoping to convert this conversation into a date. She agreed to have dinner only on the condition Winston visit her home before we went out. Lacking any paper, Bernie jotted down her number and address on the back of a photo. We both laughed because the picture was of her passed out on the beach the summer before. The good news was that we'd reconvene soon.

While I was entertaining thoughts of Bernie, Leslie and I were still roommates. We'd agreed to see other people as long as we didn't bring them home. She was searching for a new place to live and would hopefully be out of my house soon. We definitely entertained separate schedules. It would only be a matter of a few weeks before we'd be out of each other's lives. That was good news. The bad news was that Winston's last visit to unfamiliar home ended in disaster when he autographed the furniture and peed everywhere. What would I do to salvage my status with Bernie if he repeated that performance? After all the lavish praise I had given him, I'd be seen as a fraud.

On the evening of Winston's debut at Bernie's, I pulled into her driveway and there was a banner on her front door that read "Welcome Winston." Fortunately, my lecture on the way to her house proved fruitful because Winston adjusted to his new environment without incident. Our date led to future rendezvous that morphed into a growing plutonic friendship. There was authentic chemistry between us, but we agreed to keep things simple until I resolved my domestic situation at home. In time, Leslie did find an apartment and was soon to be on her own. It appeared I was about to turn a new page and start a new chapter. Unfortunately, my novel took a disastrous plot twist.

Leslie was pregnant. Apparently a night of meaningless sex in the past resulted in this disaster. I couldn't validate whether the baby was mine, but she swore she hadn't slept with anyone so the onus was on me. It was obvious our relationship was in shambles and we both knew that she wasn't ready, responsible or interested in having a child. Raising a child wasn't a viable option for either of us. So we discussed our options and decided an abortion was most practical thing to do.

Five of us were now involved with this recent set of circumstances: Leslie (being pregnant), me (because of our state of affairs), Bernie (our evolving relationship), Winston (who was anxious to be rid of Leslie), and the unborn fetus (who wasn't assigned a choice because it jettisoned ours). Leslie's moving out was suspended because she deserved my support. She was grief-stricken with guilt knowing others would give anything to have a child and she was about to abort one. She was also afraid to speak to her parents or tell her friends. At the time, she wasn't showing.

My take was that half of life just happens and the other half is how you deal with it. When you start compromising yourself and your morals for the people around you, it's probably time to change the people around you. I had no qualms with our decision. My life, liberty, peace and happiness was predicated on moving on sans child and I'll tell you why. If you're against abortion don't have one. "For those who believe in "pro-life" I respect your conviction and let's amicably concede we agree to disagree.

As human beings we've engaged in war, allowed famine and life-long poverty and made feeble attempts to really treat human life as sacred. If you support the notion of Pro Life you can't oppose healthcare for all. You can't support, or tolerate economic policies which oppress the poor, minorities, or any other marginalized group. And you cannot support unrestricted gun rights.

The real issue is whether women can make up their own mind instead of some right-wing pastor, or right-wing politician telling females what to do with their bodies. It's real easy to say you're 100% against abortion when you'll never have to make that decision. Call me crazy but this is why we chose to do what we did.

The details of managing our situation was simply a matter of making the appropriate arrangements and scheduling a date. Leslie was depressed and concerned about the lack of options concerning our situation. She became increasingly hesitant about committing to the abortion. She was a Catholic and worried about her standing with her faith. I believed in the force and held myself accountable to no one but fate. Shit happens; our destiny hides among our free choices.

Everyone grows older but does not necessarily mature. Leslie was at that transitional stage. I was sympathetic to the hardships of unfortunate circumstances because I'd been through them in the 80's. We repeatedly discussed the pros and cons of raising a child neither of us cared to rear. Eventually, she accepted the fact that life doesn't conform to your will and there are situations you can't undo. There are no erasers, it's a one act play. At some point, something's going to be taken away from you whether you like it or not (for instance, I had lost my mother only a few years earlier). Finally, Leslie got the message and we scheduled the procedure.

The next issue to address was Bernie. As a dynamic and successful business woman, she was privy to men's manipulative bullshit. They say one can play comedy, two are required for drama, but a tragedy requires three and I suspected she wasn't into threesomes. She knew how men played the game and was also aware of how to keep score. She understood the rules and was unwilling to fall victim to anyone. I anticipated she'd perceive my situation as indefensible and I was expecting the worst because she was following heroes not chasing victims. I expected losing the baby and Bernie as well.

After explaining my predicament, the erudite woman that she is politely told me to "eat shit and die," but in her own sort of elegant and classy way. My expectations were dispensed with two words, three vowels, four consonants and seven letters. The phrase is: "It's over." Welcome to Dumpsville. Population: YOU!

Several weeks later Leslie was putting distance between what had recently come to pass. She found a decent apartment on the other side of town and we were both ready to move on with our lives. When the last piece of her furniture crossed the threshold of my place, Winston sat by my side wagging his tail. His problem was resolved about her. My association with Leslie was over and Bernie and I were no longer communicating. Winston was happy and I was on my own once again. Physics can describe movement. "In life, unlike chess, the game continues after checkmate." Isaac Asimov described motion and energy, and it's true that things are always moving. It was Nikki Rowe who once said "There isn't any questioning the fact that some people re-enter your life, at the exact point of need, want or desire - it's sometimes a coincidence and most times fate." I am certain it came to me after two years and one month of meaningless encounters.

I was dining in a restaurant with my companion du jour and in walks Bernie with a man I assumed was her date. Our eyes met and I caught her startled expression. When it was convenient, I approached their table. We exchanged pleasantries and I sensed she wasn't by and large annoyed seeing me. I offered to buy them a drink, which they graciously declined. With that, I returned to my date.

Later that evening, I ruminated about my chance encounter with Bernie. With music in the background and a chardonnay in hand, I composed a letter in hopes to rekindle our friendship. It's laughable how antiquated snail mail seems to today's "Cursive Unschooled" generation. However, a written message is extremely personal and emits much more warmth than any email could ever possibly hope to do. Screw those fuck'in emoji's. There's also the added pleasure of feasting one's eyes on the writer's handwriting. Besides, it was exceedingly difficult to email in the early 90's — it didn't exist.

After several days, I followed-up and called to see whether she received my correspondence. We talked for quite some time and caught up with each other since our hiatus. To my delight, by the end of our conversation she agreed to meet me for a drink. Thirty miles and taxing schedules necessitated weekend engagements only. Of course, bringing Winston was a prerequisite when visiting her. Although she and I appreciated each other's company, I knew I was reprieved because my dog was the true object of her affection. The relationship continued to grow and everything progressed swimmingly until one weekend she came to visit me.

This particular Friday, Winston decided to take a road trip. As usual I made a half-assed attempt to track his whereabouts. When Bernie arrived Winston wasn't there to greet her. She asked where he was and I nonchalantly mentioned his expedition. All of a sudden, she went into a tirade the equivalent of a terrorist. To say she was pissed off would be an understatement. The next thing I knew, she grabbed her belongings and that was the end of our weekend. My irresponsible act ruined the weekend but clearly defined the status between me and Winston. You better believe I'd never let that happen again (at least not on the weekend).

From time to time, we quarreled and I'd leave in a huff but purposely leave Winston behind as an excuse to eventually return. She was always thrilled to have him though I can't necessarily say that about me. As our relationship evolved, we traveled to the East coast to get her friend's assessment of me and I flaunted Bernie around to my peeps in Cleveland. I began entertaining thoughts that she might be my ever-elusive knife. Not that our relationship was flawless, but our collective blemishes were exceedingly manageable.

One evening during dinner, Bernie interrupted our meal to say she had mustered up the courage to share something she'd been afraid to say since the beginning of our relationship. Nervously, I put down my utensils and pondered what could possibly be so horrible it could implode our status quo? The rolodex in my mind began considering "nuclear" situations. Could it be she committed a crime and faced incarceration? Was she terminally ill? Did she have a secret life with a family stashed away in Akron? Was she being transferred to Yugoslavia?

None of those scenarios were relationship deal breakers. Well, maybe the Akron one. Those other circumstances were manageable. Then I had this horrible epiphany she was about to say she was transgender. Not that there's anything wrong with LGBT, just that's a deal breaker for me. Ozzie's always been gender exclusive and never taken an interest in joining the pink team under any circumstances.

Finally she replied, "I've been lying about my age." Are you fucking kidding me? You can't imagine my relief after she uttered those words. To me, age is truly a mental construct. Mozart was composing at five. Einstein was 26 when he wrote the theory of relativity and Nelson Mandela was seventy-six when he became president. Oscar Wilde recognized, "I've never trusted women who told me their real age. Women who do that will tell you anything."

I immediately continued my meal and she seemed rather shocked I was so blithe about her revelation. I said, "Honey, the great thing about aging is that you don't lose any of the other ages you've been. George Burns was a boy when the Dead Sea was only sick. Age is only relevant if you make it." She seemed pleased and I was happy she was an actual woman.

We continued dating for the next few years when I decided it was time to turn the page. Making a life change can be scary but living with regret is scarier. So with that in mind, I asked Bernie if she wanted us to live together. I didn't expect that request would become such a point of contention; she wasn't certain she wanted to share herself on a full-time basis.

For whatever reason, some of us are reluctant to change. It's not that entertaining new ideas are difficult. It's that maintaining the old ones require less risk. As free-spirited as Bernie appeared, she was actually conservative when it came to change whereas my entire life's been a roller coaster ride and I believed playing it safe meant you're no longer growing. There's an axiom in AA that says if you do what you've always done, you'll get what you've always gotten.

After much consideration and the thought that Winston would be a permanent roommate, she agreed. Once again, the dog was the tipping point in my relationship with Bernie. I moved into her place and for the first time in quite a while, I was no longer the master of my domain. We married our furniture and when Bernie returned from an extended business trip, she was pleasantly surprised how I'd fused everything together. Winston was now a stable fixture and in due course, she'd figure out how to deal with me. People who say that they've met the most incredible person are only speculating because they haven't lived with them yet.

The transition wasn't spot on seamless, but it functioned very well. She traveled extensively while I also worked and maintained the house. Winston did his thing and all appeared right with the world. This routine continued for three years and then one phone call changed everything.

Although Bernie was a Midwest regional manager she was an east coast transplant and as such, answered to headquarters back in New Jersey. Because of her outstanding performance in Cleveland, she was offered an opportunity to return to the East in a corporate position with a handsome increase in pay. It was such an enticing proposal it had to be considered and also one that would define our relationship. I was content selling TV advertising in Cleveland but knew I could do that anywhere. The idea of moving East was intriguing and Winston wasn't concerned where we lived. I decided to ratchet up our relationship another notch and bought an engagement ring. I mean we'd been together several years by now and she was my Mac the Knife. So what's there to think about?

I'd been chasing women for roughly three decades. If you subtract eight years of committed relationships that leaves about 22 years of trying to get lucky. Realistically, I dated maybe six women a year, which amounts to 132 encounters. And this doesn't count the meaningful one-night stands and the blackout sex women. Thank God for Bernie because she was the last woman I hadn't dated in Cleveland. I believed in life, liberty and the happiness of pursuit. But finally I'd understood the meaning of love.

In the past, love was just a non-descriptive word until Bernie came along to give it meaning. She turned my world upside down. I shared emotions I'd never assigned to anyone else. She never slighted me and made me feel special. There was never any tension, jealousy or rivalry. I could be myself because she accepted me for me. We never needed endless conversation, because we were content in silence sharing the same space. Things that never interested me before became fascinating because I knew they interested her. I opened my heart knowing there's a chance it may be broken, but I knew I loved her. She was my best friend and possibly a soul mate to whom I could remain loyal to the end.

I asked her if she'd marry me and incredibly SHE FUCKING SAID NO!

Trying to make someone fall in love with you is as pointless as trying to nail jello to the wall. Her last guy was unfaithful and she hadn't gotten over that. Even if I was the right guy, she was wary because her last relationship ended in agony. So what makes me any different? What do you do when the person who made you feel so special yesterday makes you feel so shitty today?

It took a while to process her decision. If anger were airplane mileage, I'd be the world's number one frequent flyer. When a woman leaves a man, she's strong and independent, but when men leave women we're dickheads. Sometimes you don't know whether they're your friend, enemy or lover until it's too late. Sometimes you're all three. My pride honestly wanted to abandon her, but the problem was that I loved her. My ego was wounded because I found the one person I knew I loved and she rejected me.

Neither of us knew what to do about our quandary. She wanted to continue the relationship and wasn't ready to end it, but the offer back East was too enticing to reject. Her last long distance romance ended with the jerk that eventually dumped her for another woman. She knew I was special but just didn't want to get married. I didn't want to overreact because she didn't want a long distance romance. It came down to deciding what's worth losing and what's worth saving. We were juggling our feelings about the circumstances and carefully weighing things so as not to jeopardize what we both thought was best.

Finally, I decided to move to the East Coast and continue cohabitating but at some point, we had to tie the knot. Winston thought that was an equitable deal and so did she. However,

I told her I'd never propose to her again because there are no do overs as far as my heart is concerned. Bernie accepted her company's offer and I found employment selling TV on the East coast. We moved to a suburb outside Philadelphia and four days into our new journey, the love of both of our lives perished. Winston, who glued and sparked our live's brought us to our destination and now he left us on our own.

Death ended his life but somehow his absence enhanced ours. About a year later, Bernie and I were watching TV and out of the blue she sarcastically asked, "So when the hell do you want to get married?" How romantic!

Three months later we got married and spent the weekend in Times Square celebrating our honeymoon. Ironically, it coincided with the Westminster Kennel Club Dog Show. We mingled with some of the finest dogs in the United States. The animals were granted access to the hotels and we were able to meet them and their owners. Winston would have been happy for us. José N. Harris was right. "I think I like dogs more than I like humans. The only time a dog has ever betrayed me… was by dying."

11

JOBS

Nothing is really work unless you would rather be doing something else.
— **J. M. Barrie**

Dear Week: I've had it up to here with you. I'm going to hang with my new squeeze, Weekend. Don't even think about trying to get a hold of me for at least a few of days. I'm so over you, Love (not really) Friday. And then in the blink of an eye, Monday calls me back again.

Hello, Monday. May I ask you a question? Why are you always back so quickly? Don't you have a hobby or something, don't you ever get sick? Why can't you be a holiday once in a while? You're by far the most annoying day ending in "Y" and a terrible way to spend a 1/7th of my life. If every day is a gift, give me a receipt for Monday to exchange for another Friday. Weren't you originally named Mundane? You're like the kid that had sex for the first time and came too soon. Just once, I'd like to wake up, turn on the news and hear that Monday's been canceled and go back to sleep. You know Friday is my second favorite F word.

If that's the way you feel when Monday arrives, you're undoubtedly in the wrong job. I had to go to work on Mondays and yes, like every one of us, I hate it too, but I look at it a little differently. I don't have to work, I GET to work. I'm reasonably happy to have a job because I know a lot of folks who don't. As the weekend evaporates, I make a point to check my bank balance to see if my fortunes have changed. After recognizing my income status hasn't improved, I drive to the Gulag because I enjoy my job considerably more than being homeless.

The week in particular that I'm going to relay begins navigating horrific traffic on I-95 for the daily two hour commute (which over the week translates into a day's pay) sharing the road with the myriad of multitaskers, lane changers, women doing makeup, guys shaving, people eating or talking on phones, narcoleptics, old people, drunks and just everyday shit-for-drivers behind the wheel. It's amazing that I get to work alive. Once there, I realize I haven't had this bad of a commute since last Monday.

After surviving that nightmare, I hide in my cubicle to begin another week in a job about as exciting as a tollbooth collector. Didn't I just go through this crap last week? It's a truly dehumanizing experience where nobody gives a shit about you except what you can do to increase the company's bottom line. If assholes could fly, this place would be an airport. I will say I always give 100% at work: 15% Monday, 20% Tuesday, 25% Wednesday 20%, Thursday 15% and Friday 5%. I practice what Drew Carey preached. "Oh, you hate your job too? There's a support group for that. It's called everybody and they meet at the bar."

Most of us go through this weekly grind because we aren't members of the lucky gene pool. Our last names aren't Buffett, Gates or Koch.

The average schmuck lives pay check to pay check while the Walton (Walmart) family's wealth in 2010 was as much as the wealth of the bottom 48.8 million families in the United States, which translates to 41.5 percent of all American families. I hate when economists like Josh Givens come up with facts like this. But get mad, then get over it. Life isn't fair, but as long as we tolerate stupid people who vote against their own interests, Congress will keep letting the rich and corporations make money at our expense. Corporations are people like President Obama is a fascist Muslin. The idea that corporations can be considered human is one of the great absurdities of our time. The closest proximity to them being human beings is their ability to fuck you.

This election year, 158 households have donated almost half of all campaign money in America. If a company is considered a person under finance laws, why shouldn't they be treated the same under criminal laws? Oh, shit, I forgot. That's what why lobbyists exits. Never mind.

If I could choose my ideal place for employment I'd like a job on one the various TV crime dramas. Everyone's so enthusiastic and conscientious. No one ever calls in sick, there's never any office politics where someone's kissing up to the boss. There's no hideous or overweight people. There's never a character who isn't attractive. Where do they hide all the ugly and fat people? Everyone works in perfect harmony. No one ever finds something to complain about and nobody's obnoxious. There's never a slacker or someone who's just a complete asshole. Best of all, they solve every case in an hour. I don't know where you work, but I'm guessing it's not in a place like that.

I tolerate work out of necessity, but it seriously intrudes into my leisure time. The sad thing where I worked are the politics because no matter how much you work, there's always some asshole that works less but's paid more. I've never shied away from work and have had jobs since high school. Now that I'm in my sixties, I'm lucky to be employed with benefits. They don't pay people what I make at my age anymore. Most of us in our sixties can only find employment greeting people at Home Depot or asking if they'll have fries with their order. I'd retire tomorrow but my current employer also pays my medical benefits. I'm only a few years away from Medicare so I willing to grin and bear it.

Actually, where I'm employed today isn't that bad because it affords me time to write this book. I design ads for my current publication. It's ironic I'm here because I was actually traded to this place from another magazine where I was an account executive. The former rag had no discernible content. It was basically an ego boost for various professionals who wanted to see their pictures in a glossy publication. You've seen the kind. Each issue would focus on the top 15 doctors, lawyers, restaurants, etc. in the city. They'd get a story in exchange for advertising. Basically quid pro quo bullshit. Believe me, their egos were so big that Sarah Palin could see them from her back porch. Sprinkled in-between were car dealers and jewelry ads, the horoscopes and maybe one or two feel good stories and a few recipes. There was absolutely no reason to buy this publication. The circulation couldn't be verified and had little content.

I mentioned that I had sold radio for a station in Cleveland with huge Arbitron ratings, Cable TV with networks like ESPN, CNN, TNT with Nielsen rating, newspapers that had audit bureau circulation and this magazine didn't subscribe to anything. When people asked how many people see and read that last publication, I'd say "a lot." What I wanted to say was "shit if I know." We had nothing that validates who reads this rag. I can't even verify distribution or how many issues were printed.

The woman who owned the publication was very wealthy and needed a hobby. She'd made her money the old fashioned way—inheritance. She was a lesbian and her staff was entirely comprised of women (sans me and the guy in IT). Go figure? She was a genuine feminist who treated me equitably because she knew I couldn't care less whether she slept with women because I did, too. Different strokes for different folks. We worked together for about six months and got along swimmingly. I liked her a lot and could sense the feeling was mutual. However, my sales were awful because I couldn't find an honest hook to close many deals.

I was selling something I just didn't believe in. How can you close anyone on a product when you can't find a reason to buy it yourself? The most important rule in sales is providing value to your customer. People don't buy products they buy solutions. They don't buy a drill they buy something that makes holes. I always equated selling with dating. You walk into a bar and identify your potential customers (women). Then, you begin prospecting your base and explain your value. You get rejection after rejection after rejection and then finally you close one and seal the deal back home that night. That's how selling works. It's a numbers game.

One Friday afternoon, the magazine's owner was in her office with a man and she gestured to me to join them. You didn't have to be Nostradamus to predict what I thought what was about to happen. They say people work just hard enough to get paid and just enough not to get fired. Sales are about selling and I wasn't. I anticipated the inevitable.

Once in her office we exchanged pleasantries as I anticipated those ten dreadful words (I'm afraid we're going to have to let you go). However, to my astonishment, she introduced me to her friend (Richard) and said that I was a consummate professional, well organized and thought I'd be an asset to his company. She said he was looking for someone to design ads at his publication and she knew I had done that in the past. Sometimes the light at the end of the tunnel isn't that of an oncoming train.

The upside was that I still had a job with benefits. The down side was that this guy published a guns and ammo magazine. I'd previously created ads for a newspaper, but I also sold them, which freed me to leave the office. This job was solely in designing ads with no sales. Outside of teaching, I'd never been confined to a one room before much less stuck in a cubicle. I might as well been assigned a prison number.

I couldn't believe I'd just been traded, but after all, a job's a job and I needed to work. God bless the second amendment for permitting the right to bear arms, but I beg you people to keep those guns hidden in a safe secure place away from children. I'd prefer if it's in the same place you keep the books on evolution, tax breaks for the rich, global warming and Obamacare. When you think about it, if you're a strict constitutionalist, why do people have assault rifles and not muskets? Who cares—I got health benefits! Despite my ethical dilemma, life goes on. Besides, how many career options were left on the table at my age? In cat lives, I'd used up eight.

In a euphoric state, I said I'd be thrilled to be part of his organization and assured him that I'd add value to his company. (At least they sold a product that millions of Americans believed they needed to keep themselves safe from all those Muslim terrorists.) I knew I'd just made a pact with the devil but when you keep knocking on the Devil's door, sooner or later he'll invite you in.

I was told to report to work that next Monday. On my first day there, I noticed my colleagues were disciples of The

Fox News Network (which is generally considered the channel where truth and facts go to die). It was their station of choice in the break room. Let's be honest, Fox has championed hatemongers and miscreants for years. It's hard to take Fox seriously, but loads of low information people do because of their confused paranoia. One thing you have to hand to Fox is that they have a mantra that they regurgitate though out each program every day 24 hours a day. It was Joseph Goebbels (Hitler's minister of propaganda) who said, "The most brilliant propagandist technique will yield no success unless one fundamental principle is borne in mind constantly - it must confine itself to a few points and repeat them over and over."

I quickly realized I was in political enemy territory and had to keep my opinions close to the vest. Why would I expect my new colleagues to be liberals? They championed the NRA and one their board members is Ted Nugent, who's an embarrassment to soul patches everywhere. What a total whore I'd become for collecting a pay check from a company that contradicted my entire belief system. It reminded me of my one night romance with Skylar.

So here I am, sitting in my cubicle, waiting for someone to instruct and assign me a task. No one did for three hours. Not a single person made any effort to assist me. Around noon, Richard strolls in and assigns me to one of his minions to find something for me to do. I suddenly realized he has no clue what he has in mind for me to do. The Peter Principle crosses my mind. This man was surly and glum. You could tell by his face that his money didn't provide happiness. He earned it the old fashion way—again, through inheritance. He was in his third marriage to a much younger woman whose children were the age of his grandchildren he had with a former wife.

Finally, he summons me to his office. Once there, he explained that he's not sure what he envisions my role but he'll have a better idea before the week is over. With that, I was dismissed. There were a few ads to design but not enough for a forty hour week. The majority of the advertisements came from agencies. I figured he'd have me preform other duties to compensate.

Now I'm confined in my prison cell otherwise known as a cubicle deciding how to entertain my day. Possible choices included downloading porn, tracking the internet or interacting with my homies on Facebook. Those choices seemed counterproductive so I decided to pursue something I'd never had the time to do—write a book. In a way, what seemed to be lemons I turned into lemonade. Richard had given me a grant to write a book.

As days turned into weeks and weeks became months he had me doing an assortment of tasks from designing ads, calling clients, emailing former clients and other menial duties, which I did willingly. Basically, I was nothing more than a secretary. He barely gave me the time of day and rarely engaged me. I was baffled that I was even on his payroll. I was a year away from Medicare so I decided to see how long this charade could continue. As Nietzsche once said, "He who has a 'why' to live for can bear almost any how."

Richard was involved in so many other endeavors, the magazine was just one of his hobbies. He rarely came into the office before noon and when he showed up I'd wonder now that he's here who was running hell? What most annoyed me about him was when he'd walk into my cubicle and ask what I was doing while I was in mid-sentence talking with a customer he'd tap me on the shoulder to garner my attention. At times, he displayed a nasty temper directed at his employee's subject to his mood that day. He's what you'd call a triple threat boss: angry, mean and rude. But other than that, a real delightful guy. Everyone knows what the nickname for Richard is. Need I say more?

It's amazing what you'll stomach to collect a paycheck and sorry to say I needed benefits so I tolerated his nonsense. I did as much as possible to stay out of his way. Many of my colleagues were from the South Philly area, which isn't exactly a bastion of affluence, diversity or open-mindedness. It's been said that your perspective on life springs from the cage you've been held captive. It's been my experience to note that people who are unhappy with their station in life scapegoat and assign blame to others because of their own miserable plight.

A lot of people who are pro-gun are also anti anyone who thinks and doesn't look like them. I inherited a work place with low information consumers who daily condemn the atrocities in the world on the Islamic, illegitimate and fascist president. In their eyes, he's the culprit taking their country away from them. It's always Obama's fault. Just the other day, I heard Barack was the assassin behind the "grassy knoll."

During the week, I provided a colleague a ride to the bus stop on my way home. He's a White divorced Vietnam veteran with two grown sons still living in his house in the ghetto. He's also living pay check to paycheck to make ends meet. All he ever said on our way to the bus stop was how the Nigger president was ruining the country and made his life worse. But what would you expect from an unfortunate loser? His sentiments of bigotry and ignorance were manifested because of his own predicament in life. We like to think we control our destiny, but fate isn't fickle for nothing. Much luck lies in opportunity. All you can do is play the cards dealt to you and hope for the best. Until this job, I've never been confined to a cubicle. It is the most restrained I've ever been. If you intend becoming an accountant, banker, receptionist, or administrative assistant then yeah, have at it. The only reason I tolerated this job is because I looked at it as a grant to write. It's all about perspective, think about the lobsters on the Titanic when it sank. I've never let work explain who I am.

Usually when meeting a stranger, as a conversation starter the question asked, "So tell me about yourself?" More often than not, the stranger will talk about a job as if it defines them. What you do isn't who you are. Just because you're a lawyer doesn't necessarily mean you're an asshole. If you've got no interests outside of work and can't converse without referring to something work related, then you've confused making a 'living' with having a life.

Success isn't about converting your signature into an autograph. A lot of those people are douche bags — look at Donald Trump. Can you honestly tell me Kim Kardashian actually works? Here's a person who makes a living by opening her mouth and saying, "Well what is my talent?" Well, a bear can juggle and stand on a ball and he's talented, but he's not famous. Folks, life isn't fair.

Once you become worm food, the score's tied unless you believe in reincarnation. In reality, the "stuff" you've accumulated is simply bupkis. My existence is based on enjoying life while residing on this side of the dirt. This isn't Hotel California because at any time you WILL eventually leave.

In sixty plus years, I've been employed as a delivery boy, professional singer, clothing salesman, camp counselor, school teacher, text book agent, board game inventor, drug dealer, telephone booth manufacturer, pay phone purveyor, construction foreman, account executive in radio, cable TV, magazines, newspapers, an alarm security consultant, a gutter salesman, substitute teacher and most recently a stranger in a strange land in Philadelphia as an ad designer. I guess you could say I've had a varied background, a jack-of-all-trades and master of none.

a year shy of Medicare, nominated me as one of Mitt
_y's fabled 47% not worthy of his time. You know the
: dependent and victims the government has responsibility
to care for, entitled to health care, food and housing. I'm
supposedly one of the folks who pays no income tax. Of course,
the ideal situation is for the government to live within its own
means and not yours. What amazes me is that the Romneys
or Trumps don't understand that the only thing separating
their privilege and entitlement from someone like me is the
lucky gene pool. They give arrogance a bad name. Maybe that
accounts for why the Hawaiian's still dining off the White
House china and they're searching for other people to offend.

Of all the jobs I've ever chased, there were a couple that
stood out the most: one I created myself and the other I never
got because of the illegitimacy of the system. Behind the wheel
of my automobile driving back to Cleveland in the summer
of 79 and while sharing a joint with my friend Robby, I had
this epiphany and said, "Wouldn't it be great to sell something
about drugs without the risk of dealing them?"

The previous year Paramount Pictures released the classic
movie "Up in Smoke" about two stoners who unknowingly
smuggle a van - made entirely of marijuana from Mexico
to L.A. It featured Cheech and Chong and grossed over 44
million dollars. The movie's success was the vision how we
could market something pot related and cash in. My inkling
was to make a board game called "Pot Luck." It would be a
knockoff of Monopoly except the object of the game was to
become the wealthiest marijuana dealer.

All of our friends smoked dope, so we wanted to provide
them entertainment while they were enjoying their buzz. By
chance, Robby's father-in-law owned a printing business, loved
the idea and was willing to help. Here's how the game worked.

Each player received a marker to navigate the board, which began on the "Straight Spot." After rolling the dice and you happened to land on a pot space, you had the option to purchase it for the price of a pound of that particular herb. You increased its value by adding more pounds on that space. There were 20 varieties of weed ranging from Colombian, Jamaican, Hawaiian, Just Good Pot, as well as a host of others. When you purchased the space, you obtained a deed with a picture of the pot and its street value on the front with a history of the herb on the back.

When another player landed on your pot space, they paid a "toking fee." This was how you accrued money. Beside the pot spaces, there were several others that were pertinent to the daily activities of a drug dealer. Our initial run was 10,000 units and we began an advertising campaign. We targeted games to the top twenty-five newspapers, and a few magazines like Rolling Stone, High Times and Playboy. We sent games to program directors at AOR (album oriented rock) stations. We also acquired a list of "Head Shops" around the country which became our best source of distribution. We even sent a game to Cheech and Chong (they never acknowledged receipt).

We purchased ads in High Times Magazine — overnight, the game was in nearly every state in America. Some people mailed pot to us. We graciously accepted their donations and unlike Bill Clinton, we inhaled. There was an annual boutique and fashion show in New York that included paraphernalia dealers who sold bongs and pipes, rolling papers, incense, scales, tee shirts, leather goods and rock posters. One booth sold a cocaine additive product that was displayed with giant mountains of white powder on their table. It looked like cocaine and the people who passed their booth snorted their product hoping to catch a buzz.

We were fortunate enough to land a meeting with the people who owned EZ Wider rolling papers. Our objective was to exchange a percentage of the game's profits for ad space inside the flap of their papers. Unfortunately, we were rejected because they alleged their product was used exclusively to roll tobacco and our game would suggest something otherwise. Later that evening, we attended a party thrown by some of the vendors from the show. As soon as we arrived, we smelled the pungent aroma of marijuana intoxicating the room. People were rolling joints and much to our shock, they were using EZ Widers rolling papers. Those fuckin' roller paper dudes lied to us! Is nothing sacred?

In spite of the setback of the EZ Wider rejection, we managed to sell all 10,000 units from the ads in High Times and our network of head shops throughout the country. Because of our success, we decided to manufacture more games.

Shortly after producing another run of 10,000 units, the most horrific nightmare occurred. Ronald Reagan moved to 1600 Pennsylvania Avenue and the First Lady embraced an anti-drug campaign. To promote her agenda, Nancy met with school children in Oakland and declared: "Drugs take away the dreams from every child's heart and replace them with a nightmare, and it's time in America to stand up and replace those dreams." A little girl raised her hand and asked, "Mrs. Reagan, what do you do if somebody offers you drugs?" Nancy replied, "Just say 'No!'" This simple phrase became a mantra which persisted, in various forms, for years.

If she'd only said: "Sex, drugs, rock & roll; pills, hash and weed. Life's a bitch and then you die, so fuck the world and let's get high," our distribution network to head shops wouldn't have vanished. For those too young to have patronized one of these establishments, a head shop was a retailer specializing in paraphernalia used for consumption of tobacco and new age herbs, as well as counterculture art, magazines, music, and clothing. They also sold pipes, bongs, cigarette clips, rolling papers, scales, black lights, posters, incense, cigarette lighters, and... MY FUCKIN' GAME!

Because of the First Lady's crusade, pressure was put on these establishments and they began closing head shops at an alarming rate. We were on the verge of signing a deal with Spencer Gifts with an initial test order of 25,000 units but because of dear Nancy that deal fell through. I'd envisioned having a beautiful relationship with every shopping mall in America, instead my dream ended unexpectedly. Shortly thereafter, I was embellishing my resume seeking new employment. Six months later, I substituted my jeans and tennis shoes for fancy ties and suits selling sixty-second commercials at a rock station in Cleveland.

So that job I created for myself was great. What infuriated me about the demise of Robby and my efforts came at the expense of a woman who promoted a war on drugs while her husband sanctioned the CIA dealing cocaine to the American public! (Short reminder: In 1998, the CIA admitted to allowing cocaine trafficking to take place by Nicaragua Contras using facilities and resources supplied by the US government. Marine Lieutenant Colonel Oliver North was involved, indicted and initially convicted to a few years and $150,000 in fines for following orders.)

Although my possible fortune vanished, the game provided several amusing anecdotes. I experienced a situation similar to a scene from Woody Allen's "Annie Hall," where the actor overhears an academically self-important film professor citing the action while waiting in line to get into a movie, not knowing Woody's there. I attended a party and stumbled across a group of people playing Pot Luck. I noticed two players arguing over the rules. They screamed at each other insisting their position was correct. I felt obliged to resolve their dispute, so I approached them and injected my opinion. One of the players (clearly intoxicated) sprung up from his chair and said, "How the fuck do you know?" I paused for a second and responded, "Because I'm the guy who invented the GAME!" After examining the box, he realized that my name matched the one on my driver's license and quietly sat down. You can't imagine the "shit-eating grin" on my face while exiting the room. It really doesn't get any better than that.

The job I didn't get was the one that I really wanted. I was fifty four at the time and laid off from my account executive position. Finding new ad jobs in the market were scarce and generally politically allocated. My contacts from Ohio didn't translate to eastern Pennsylvania, so I had a limited network. For the money I was making, there were loads of twenty- and thirty-something's who they could hire for much less. In spite of those obstacles I gave it my best effort, but failed to land another TV gig.

My teaching degree had expired several years earlier. I never renewed it as I was chasing various pipe dreams. I was a seasoned account executive who no one was eager to hire. I wasn't at the Willie Loman stage, but there comes a time when you ask yourself, "what would satisfy you during the course of your day?" I knew teaching was my true calling so I discarded ad sales and began substitute teaching.

It had been quite a while since I'd walked into a classroom and I wasn't sure whether I was still relevant. After all, I could be these kid's grandfather. There was a clear generation gap and I wasn't certain I could bridge that. Nonetheless, I began substituting. A substitute has about five minutes to establish control of a classroom. These kids don't know you and recognize you're not the arbitrator of their grade. In essence, you're the target for their abuse and amusement. Fortunately for me, I still had what it takes to command a classroom.

Over time, I established solid relationships with the administrators in several districts. A few systems had an opening for the fall and suggested I renew my certificate to qualify for a permanent position. With that, I began my recertification journey. What a nightmare! After complying with their request, I received a letter from the Department of Education which informed me I'd not met the 2.8 GPA requirements and rejected me. If I wanted to appeal, I could petition the Secretary of Education's Certificate Appeal Committee. My college GPA was 2.5, which I thought was respectable considering I was stoned half the time, protesting the Vietnam War, working a part time job, attending lectures, studying and chasing women. I was multi-tasking before there was such a thing. Doesn't that count for something?

Despite this set back, I wasn't about to give up my quest to teach so I did petition the appeals committee and was granted an audience to plead my case. I began researching to strengthen my appeal and uncovered a few intriguing pieces of information. The first is what's called "grade inflation," which was the process of awarding higher grades today for work that would have received lower marks in the past. Then, I learned that George W. Bush had a 2.35 GPA when he graduated from Yale in 1968.

How is it that the President of the United States is qualified to direct foreign policy, negotiate treaties, nominate judges to the Supreme Court, command the military, veto legislation and be accountable for the nuclear football yet be incapable of teaching 11th grade American History in Pennsylvania? (Although I will admit, the only difference between George W. and 11th graders is that 11th graders can't find Iraq on a map and he couldn't find a way to get out of there.)

After several weeks, the day arrived to confront the appeals committee. I confidently entered the building and was ushered into a chamber that resembled a courtroom. There were about a dozen board members who introduced themselves. I was allotted fifteen minutes to give my presentation and as any smart instructor I came prepared with a 12 page statement I'd created and gave them each a copy. These were my lesson plans for today's class.

The crux of my argument focused on grade inflation and its blatant abuse over the past several decades. I presented graph charts highlighting my position, which flummoxed the majority of the board. They looked at this information as if this was something they'd never seen. When I presented the question about the president failing the requirement to meet their academic standards, the sound of throat clearing resounded.

By the end of my performance, a few members made their concocted phony baloney comments extolling my efforts and informed me they'd respond to my plea in due time. I thought my presentation went well. Not once did I insinuate that they appeared to be holier than thou pompous assholes, pretentious snobs or arrogant bureaucrats. I wondered which face they saw when they looked into the mirror because words mean nothing when your behavior is entirely the opposite. Six weeks later I received the committee's decision. They determined that I didn't meet all statutory and regulatory requirements for the certification and my appeal was denied. Well, so much for teaching again. You know I don't care if they'd peed in my Cheerios, rained on my parade and short sheeted my bed simultaneously. What could have been was not to be.

That left me in my cubical going through the motions as an ad designer. It isn't what I envisioned 40 years ago. So riddle me this Batman, the question that Justin Alcala posed: "Which is the true nightmare, the horrific dream that you have in your sleep or the dissatisfied reality that awaits you when you awake?"

Making money isn't difficult in itself; what's hard is to make it doing something worth doing. I think most of us are looking for a mission, not a job. Sometimes we do what we have to do, until we're able to do what we'd like to do and often that never happens. Just never get too busy making a living you forget to make a life.

Ironically, the week I finished the last chapter of my manuscript coincided with the week Richard let me go. I guess he intended me to work for him to find a passion to do something, which was to write a book. Thanks, Dick, for providing me with my new career as author. You've just made Mondays just another day of the week. Good bye, I-95, I won't miss you.

12

AN OLD MAN'S RANT

It's paradoxical that the idea of living a long life appeals to everyone, but the idea of getting old doesn't appeal to anyone.
— **Andy Rooney**

At some point, everyone has to come to terms with time as George Carlin said "You become twenty-one... turn thirty... push forty, reach fifty and make it to sixty. After that you hit seventy and then it's a day by day thing; you hit lunch." Joplin, Hendrix and Morrison all died at 27. Princess Diana at 36, Steve Jobs at 56, Prince at 57 and Keith Richards is still playing "Satisfaction." Go figure? Somehow 17 fast-tracked to 65 overnight.

There's a certain freedom being sixty five. You're afforded the opportunity to look beyond the role society has asked you to play. You assign time and reposition your priorities accordingly. Most of the important questions in life have been answered, yet what lies ahead is a mystery. As each day, evolves I try to make sense of a senseless world and it becomes abundantly clear that one's health means everything. You're only sure of today, so I try not to be cheated out of it.

My new calling is taking care of my wife. She's spent the past year recovering from two hip replacements and recent spine surgery. At this time in our lives, Jackie Mason's mantra is true. "It's no longer a question of staying healthy. It's a question of finding a sickness you like." So far, the only difficulty with retirement is not looking forward to having a day off. It gives a whole new meaning to weekends. All things considered, I can live with that.

I'm no longer as concerned about my appearance. My hair is turning gray and so be it. I'd like to be thinner, but I'm content fitting in the clothes I have. I'm delighted I don't have to shave daily and often wear the same outfit the next day. Who cares if my socks match? I answer to no one except my wife and Simon, our dog.

About a year ago, I reunited with Ozzie who had forsaken me a while back, as I mentioned. Out on his own, he discovered he wasn't as clever as he thought. He wasn't getting lucky anymore and was aging poorly, so he took Cialis to step up his game. Unfortunately, he sustained a nine hour erection and had a mild stroke. Begging for forgiveness, he pleaded with me to take him back and like the sap I am I did. He no longer dictates the agenda. Free at last, free at last.

I live in an affluent zip code, our finances are relativity solid, my health's okay and there's harmony within my family. Each day, I'm grateful that I'm divorced from the politics and chaos around the globe. My serenity comes from keeping things in their proper prospective.

According to research on globalissues.org, almost half the planet lives on less than $2.50 a day and at least 80% of humanity lives on less than $10 a day. Think about that next time you buy a bottle of wine or go to the car wash. Why in the world should I complain? A lot of people have it so much worse than me. It's all relative.

After six decades I'm amazed I'm still on this side of the dirt. Three of my uncles passed in their fifties and my mom literally died in my arms at sixty. I hope to grow old at a snail's pace and pray there's nothing left to learn the hard way. Throughout it all, I've learned that reality is life without a net or eraser. It's hard to be an idealist once your innocence is gone. Gilda Radner once said, "Some poems don't rhyme... some stories don't have a clear beginning, middle, and end. Life's about not knowing, having to change, taking the moment and making the best of it, without knowing what's going to happen next."

Being exists linearly, physically, and mentally. You're born, you age, and along the way you feel. The only constant in the equation is change. I was taught to respect my elders, and now I'm old enough I don't have to respect anyone. I brought recklessness to my marriage and my wife gave me sanity. I'm a lucky man. I just have to remind myself to stop thinking like a "grumpy old man." The awkward parts of life are behind me, but somehow I can't shake being a "cranky" S.O.B.

I've navigated adolescence, adult anxiety, disastrous career decisions, and countless relationships with fond memories. There's a secure roof over my head and nothing's raining down on me. I've noticed the volume knob turns left and appreciate that love has nothing to do with expecting what to get but instead knowing how to give. I listen to less music, watch fewer sporting events and consume less TV. Laugh track comedies, singers, dancers, housewives, bachelors, or survivors don't interest me. I mainly watch the news because I need something to get pissed about.

Rarely do I attend concerts because venues are too large and tickets are astronomically overpriced. Unless Elvis, Hendrix or Joplin return, I'll pass. You'd have to pay me to go to a mall. I've already bought everything I really need. Besides, everything's a knock off of something I bought several years ago. My cell phone has two apps: on and off and its rotary dial. I guess that's why I'm not in anyone's demo except the medical companies.

Let me ask you this: if dying meant leaving the stage long enough to trade outfits and return as a new person would you retreat back to yesterday or rush into tomorrow? The beauty of today is that you can count on it not lasting forever.

Gone are the computer-less days when the world lived in slow motion. Technology's fashioned a social and mental shift waiting for us to assign it form. It's created ambiguous boundaries between reality and fantasy. The question you have to ask is: are we being controlled by these devices or are these devices controlling us? Do you really have to take that call? Can't it wait? What the fuck's so important?

The other day, I asked my 27 year old niece how many friends she had and she causally said 1200. I was perplexed because I only have ten friends although I do have several acquaintances on social media. I asked if she really believed they were genuine friends and she answered yes. Then, I retrieved a legal pad and asked her to jot down the names of her most preferred hundred colleagues and she professed she couldn't.

Somehow she hasn't discovered that lasting relationships are with flesh-and-blood contacts and she perceives intimacy as a virtual embrace. I'll never understand how online communication didn't include offline activities, but that's how relationships are in the 21st century.

I actually don't live in this century, I'm only visiting but I'd like to know who put a "stop payment" on my reality check? The truth may suck but it doesn't go away. After you've heard two different versions of the same eye witnessed event, you worry about history.

rew up in the world without Google. I may be wrong, but I believe facts aren't fantasy and shouldn't be divorced from reality. I've watched history unfold in real time. Just because I'm getting old doesn't mean I have amnesia. I'm getting too old for this nonsense. Time has changed me but I can't change time. I've reached the crescendo of rage, knowing the deck's stacked, the fix is in and greed's undermining what's right.

I've lived through the cold war, the moon landing; Watergate, women's liberation, the war on drugs; gay rights and five major American military conflicts. Please, stop bullshiting me.

I watched Superbowl I and the other forty nine. I've listened to vinyls of Sinatra, 8-tracks of the Beatles, cassettes of Donna Summer, CD's of Prince and today recoil as young people download Justin Bieber and Kanye West. Time's passed so quickly that the New Kids on the Block are the old men on the cul de sac.

I was in a draft lottery without the right to vote being asked to fight in Vietnam where old fat white men sent black people to fight Asian people to protect the country they stole from the Native Americans. I've watched the planet double, survived the Cuban Missile crisis and lived through the civil rights movement, the murders of JFK, Martin Luther King as well as Bobby Kennedy. I watched Neil Armstrong's step foot on the moon and a year later, observed the slaughter of four of my classmates at Kent State.

I was around when Nixon resigned and Gerald Ford became President without a single citizen casting a ballot. I also saw nine Judges negate 150 million votes and put George W. Bush in the oval office. Now that's real Democracy!

In my time, a pope was shot, the Cold War ended, schools were desegregated, women were given the right to choose what to do with their bodies, corporations become people and same sex marriage became law. I lived long enough to see America elect a president judged by his character in spite of his color. And now I watch in astonishment and agree wholeheartedly with Johnathan Giftos (who posted this on his FB page):

> ...a faithfully married President who was the son of a single mother, the first Black editor of Harvard Review and a professor of Constitutional Law is considered unintelligent, immoral and anti-American by the right, while a xenophobic, misogynistic, "serial philandering", trust fund kid who quotes from the National Enquirer, peddles conspiracy theories, routinely calls women ugly and fat, calls McCain a loser for having been a prisoner of war and who has advocated torture and bombing of women and children has captured the hearts of a majority of Republicans.

As much as we thought that race and gender issues were behind us, it's been quite the contrary. We murder black people for failing to use turn signals and conservatives promote overturning Roe vs. Wade. Can someone explain to me how Corporations are people? Why does a deflated football command more attention than the Senate not willing to do their job and fill a vacant seat in the Supreme Court?

Have we always been this foolish or is now a special moment? I've had it up to here with people's religion repudiating gay marriage. If you don't like gay marriage blame straight people who keep having gay babies. And who in the world believes building walls will keep Mexicans from crossing the border? They fuck'in BUILD TUNNELS!

Right wing fanatics constantly talk about taking this country back and I ask myself where it went? I checked my

GPS and it appears to be exactly where it's always been. Maybe I never got an Amber alert. When did the United States disappear? Should we start somewhere in the 21th century or regress to the beginning of the republic? Let's use 1946 when the Pledge of Allegiance didn't contain the phrase "under God"? How about 1863 when "in God we trust" wasn't on our coins. Would 1857 be suitable when Black people were deemed property or possibly 1830 when Andrew Jackson appropriated the Indian Removal Act?

Maybe, just maybe, and this is just a wild guess, they're referring to 2008 when 66 million Americans elected a Kenyan, Muslim, fascist, Marxist, lying, not-like-one-of-us President. You know their ilk. They're the people who identify themselves with the core values of white supremacy. I guess they've haven't heard that the seat assignments on the bus have been rearranged and anyone can sit in the front.

While we're having this conversation about taking things back, there are a few matters I'd prefer we exchange. I'd like America to re-claim the integrity of the news media when they weren't required to generate revenue and actually deliver relevant information. I'd like so-called journalist's to hold politicians accountable and refuse to let them obfuscate questions; make them provide legitimate answers. Understand that 90% of the media is controlled by six companies. Fifteen of the terrorists responsible for the 911 attacks were from Saudi Arabia, and Prince Alwaleed (a Saudi) owned several shares of stock in News Corp, which runs Fox news. Wake up people; Democracy isn't a spectator sport. You have to pay attention.

I'd like schools to reinstitute civics classes. I'd like to go back to the FCC enforcing the fairness doctrine act. I'd like to repeal Citizen's United. I'd like to see term limits in Congress and prohibit any former congress person becoming a lobbyist. I'd like to establish a truth jar, where every politician would have to contribute a thousand dollars every time they misstated, messaged and distorted the facts. We'd reduce the federal deficit in no time at all.

Each generation is merely old words reborn with new faces and ideas. The "Greatest" one fought World War I and were realists. The "Silent" one fought Hitler and were idealists. The "Boomers" lived through Vietnam and political assassinations and may be responsible for all the turmoil today. They thought they could change the world but fell somewhere between their parents' idealism and their children's eighties cynicism. The "X'ers" were Latch Key Kids, slackers and the MTV generation hated rules and didn't respect authority.

"Millennials" are rule followers; overindulged by their parents, who inherited terrorist attacks and two wars. They graduated college in a recession and accrued tons of debt. It's likely they'll never acquire the financial surplus, employment stability and material possessions of their parents did.

Now we have "Generation Z" kids who came out of the womb with computers, social media, multitasking and process information without understanding substance. We're all defined by the time zone in which we live. No matter which zone you reside our strengths as a nation lie in our differences. As time passes, the more I know the less I understand, which makes sense because the more you know the more you have to consider. In my case, it's because of my intellectual curiosity. I'm not saying I'm smart, I'm just inquisitive. That's why I'm a cynic. My constitution isn't structured in relation to winning and losing, because while the game's being played, I'm essentially ahead or behind. Winning and losing is determined once the contest is over and as long as I'm breathing, I can affect the outcome.

For the "clueless" I offer these modest words of wisdom. It's time to lose those impudent smiles, delete some apps, stop texting and tweeting silly nonsense, and put the asinine phone down. Take the buds out of your ears, turn your caps around to face forward, tie your sneakers, and pull your pants above your ass crack. Get rid of those incriminating pictures you posted on Facebook.

Understand that as deft you think you are at multi-tasking, it's impossible to be proficient doing several things at once. Focus on executing one task exceptionally. Stop abbreviating words and learn to spell. Eliminate the expressions "totally," "like," "awesome," "OMG" and "BFF" from your vocabulary. It's compulsory that you increase your attention span and appreciate news as more than sound bites and one hundred and forty characters. The Internet will provide every aspect of any issue, but it's your job to evaluate, and determine whether it's factually correct. Wikipedia isn't the most definitive source of truth and you can't rely on cliff notes. Research is essential.

Realize "YouTube" squanders time and gets in the way of productive thought. Xbox is the work of the devil, it successfully distracts you from those who will exploit your interests. Don't presume you're entitled to everything just because you think you merit it. Your parents spoiled you. They didn't mean to, they just couldn't help themselves. There's no manual for raising children. They did the best they thought they could. Now "you" must step up. Whatever you do, always give 100%, unless you're donating blood. There's no such thing as a "free lunch" even though you download porn and listen to music for nothing. Credit card companies capitalize off your instant gratification. You'll ultimately be expected to pay, and undoubtedly be held accountable.

By the way, bankruptcy laws are more draconian than ever. If you think nobody cares that you're alive, try missing a couple of credit card payments. Bankruptcy lawyers expect to be paid.

Relationships aren't hook ups, friends with benefits, getting lucky, monkey sex, silly pictures on websites, and more than holding hands. Brittany at twenty won't look and be the same at forty-five unless you recognized her inner beauty from the start. Outer beauty is time sensitive and recedes with age.

True love is based on whether you like yourself, your compassion for others, and tenuously connected to orgasms. Understand that your life partner is your best friend, unwavering companion and trustworthy barometer who'll tell you that your shit smells, covers your back, and loves you in spite of yourself.

It's impossible to accumulate 1300 friends unless you can name them all. No one really gives a rat's ass that you just bought a new pair of jeans at the mall and why in the fuck do I need to see what you ate at a restaurant? Compensate people for providing you entertainment. They deserve it for providing you joy.

Chances are you won't have a better life than your parents because Washington lobbyists are blowing your politicians to finance agendas which aren't in your best interests. Reality's about paying bills, making ends meet, raising a family, global disasters, repressive regimes, politics and wars. Don't confuse this with the nonsense about housewives in any city, bachelors or bachelorettes or ubiquitous people like Kim Kardashian who are simply famous for being famous.

There aren't actual vampires or zombies and superheroes don't wear costumes; they're regular people like the ones who sacrificed their lives to stop the terrorist's in Shanksville, Pennsylvania. Some heroes do wear uniforms, like pilot Sully Sullenberger who saved one hundred-fifty-four people on flight 1549 by just doing his job.

Stop confusing exposure with accomplishment. Justin Bieber is ubiquitous, but Steve Jobs changed your life; know the difference. Arrest the notion that brand names promote your status. Your desire and want is a combination of peer pressure and clever marketing. Question those pretending to represent your interests and examine their motives and funding sources. Believe nothing without investigation and if it doesn't agree with your own logic and common sense, don't trust it.

People of color, stop pretending you're a conservative Republican by advancing the talking points of old fat white men. They despise you, and wish it was 1950 when everyone had assigned seats and knew their place. Your chocolate face is nothing more than a prop for Fox news. The United States of America has an astounding history of murdering people of color. Just know that you can be pulled over and murdered for Driving While Black. Black people have lived their whole lives in a dream world, except it's been a nightmare. Ask any of your relatives. For God's sake, study history and realize that you weren't' a part of "We the People" when the Declaration of Independence was written.

Recognize your right to have an opinion was established by those who sat in the back of the bus and were sprayed with fire hoses, bitten by dogs and marched for your civil rights. A lot of folks did some heavy lifting for the opportunities you have today.

There will be people who will say you're not good enough and maybe they're right. But don't take no for an answer. Seek the career you want and pursue any goal. Surround you self with people who act their age and not their shoe size.

You have to decide whether you want to change the status quo somehow, or navigate around it to find a happy medium. Until then treat every day as if it may be your last and make the most of it. Don't worry about what others think of you even if they think you're crazy because maybe you are. Just remember that in this life you're on your own. Your exhilarating insanity lets others dream outside of the lines and become who they're destined to be. And remember, only dead fish go with the flow.

ABOUT THE BOOMER

R. Winston Carroll

I was born in Cleveland Ohio in 1950. I've performed a myriad of jobs and today have the good fortune to be retired and live in Bucks County Pennsylvania with my wonderful wife Bernie and my rescue dog Simon. Of the many careers I've had, there were times I earned six figures and times I lived from paycheck to paycheck. This has given me an interesting perspective on the disparity between how the have and the have-not's live. I speak to everyone the same way whether they're a trash collector or the Queen of England. The bona fide sign of a person's character is how one treats someone who can't advance your agenda, and how you address those who can't fight back. I've always believed there's a difference between making a living and having a life. I deem time more valuable than money because time can't be purchased. I may not have gone where I intended to go, but I think I've ended up where I need to be.

My political DNA leans left and I've never been fond of rules. I am free because I know I am morally responsible for what I do. I look at life through kaleidoscope eyes with a sense of amazement. It's been my experience that life is divided into genres; some horrific, others romantic, some tragic and others amusing.

If life were merely simple, that would be easy. If it were challenging, it wouldn't be a problem. But I wake up each day torn between a desire to improve the world and a desire to enjoy the world. I endorse Einstein's belief that "Two thing are infinite, the universe and human stupidity and I'm not sure about the universe. Just maybe this world might be another planets hell, but an intelligent hell would be a better place than a stupid paradise.